Jack Kershaw
Attorney at Law
3616 Doge Place
Nashville, Tennessee 37204
(615) 292-2316

"Dear George:

If I may so address you.

You had me laughin' out loud—and all the time I was completely unaware that I was an actor in such a fine morality play!

Best regards,

Jack"

(Jack Kershaw,
"Mr. Naked," from the short story *Pony*)

"This is the subject for Mr. Naked in 'Pony'"

DAVIDSON COUNTY

KERSHAW, Jack—Age 97, died Tuesday, September 7, 2010. Artist, sculptor, home builder, farmer, lawyer, lecturer, southern historian, Vanderbilt Graduate in the early 1930's. A renaissance man, non conforming in both dress and content. Jack was one of those unforgettable characters portrayed in the Readers Digest Articles. A gold plated eccentric. Jack was born in Missouri in 1913 to Karl and Ethel Norton Kershaw. His father had a degree in geology and civil mining. His mother was born in Wyoming and after her mother's death, her father abandoned his four children. Her uncle took the boys and raised them in Wyoming and Jack's mother and sister were sent to live with an aunt in Tennessee. She was raised in a home of privilege and received a good education, becoming a school teacher. She met and married Karl Kershaw in Missouri, and from this union Jack was born. Karl moved his family to Old Hickory, TN when WWI broke out, and was the engineer in charge of building the DuPont power plant. Mrs. Kershaw returned to the classroom to teach. Jack attended Warner school, MBA where he played football, and attended a military school at Stone Mountain, GA and then Vanderbilt University where he played football while majoring in geology, history and art. When the first pro football team was formed in Nashville in the late 1930's, he was the quarter back playing with such notable local characters as Haynes Noel. This team was dissolved due to the war. Jack was a member of the State of Tennessee Militia as a Calvary member. He was a member of the first Tennessee Arts Commission. Jack became associated with a group of intellectuals who called themselves the Fugitive Poets of Vanderbilt in the 1920's. This group of students would go on to make a great impact of how the history of the south would be told. The Fugitive is considered to be one of the most influential publications in the history of American letters. The Fugitives made Vanderbilt a fountainhead of the New Criticism, the dominant mode of textual analysis in English during the first half of the twentieth century. Included in this group among the most notable Fugitives were John Crowe Ransom, Allen Tate, John Crow, Merrill Moore, Donald Davidson, William Ridley Wills, Robert Penn Warren, Andrew Lytle, Cleanth Brooks, and the poet Laura Riding, although not a member was

DAVIDSON COUNTY

West Tennessean Jesse Hill Ford. Andrew Lytle was a first cousin of Jack's late wife. Jack was married to Mary Noel in the 1930's taking up residence in the former Glendale Country Clubhouse, which had closed during the depression and owned by his father-in-law, Edwin Noel. Mary was from an equally privileged family and an educated southern dame. It could be said they were equals as she was raised into art, music and letters. Mary died in 1989. Mr. Noel owned a very large block of land in south Nashville. He and Jack farmed and developed this property. Jack and Mary decided, more on a "lark" to attend the YMCA LAW School. He was admitted to the bar in the 1960's. His most famous client was the late James Earl Ray. Jack has written, but yet not published a book on all involved in this affair. Because of the sensitive nature of its contents, is being kept at a secure off site from his home. He has two other yet unpublished works set for release sometime in the future. A practical jokester, his antics in the court room by his such coconspirators' as the late Dave and J.W. Rutherford, Dan Garfincle, Sam Wallace and Judge Zuccarella are legendary. His most notable art piece is that of General Nathan Bedford Forrest Horse and Rider, located on I-65 South just north of Brentwood, and Joan of Arch, a two story depiction of her death at the stake. Jack was a co-founder of the League of the South; member of the (SCV) Sons of Confederate Veterans; M.O.S.B. the officer corps of the SCV; member Joe Johnston Camp 28 SCV. He was an heir of Admiral Kershaw CSA of South Carolina. Jack is survived by two 2nd cousins, Mike Jamison of Los Angeles, CA and Debra Pronto of Indianapolis, IN and his cat Coco. Jack had many friends that have looked after him these last two years, Ryan and Terry Reeves of Old Hickory. Others in Jack's inter circle of close friends were Frank Ritter, Ross Massey, Wes Shofner, Henry Hood and Sir William Dorris. Jack's wishes of cremation have been carried out. Celebrations of Remembrances set for September 18th at 11 a.m., at All Saints Southern Episcopal Church, 46th and Park Avenue, West Nashville, with Father Huron Manning presiding at the church. MOUNT OLIVET FUNERAL HOME, (615) 255-4193.

Mount Olivet
FUNERAL HOME & CEMETERY

9-17-10

Jack Kershaw
Attorney at Law
3616 Doge Place
Nashville, Tennessee 37204

"Jack Kershaw is Mr. Naked in my short story 'Pony'"

Mr. George Spain
1724 N. Observatory
Nashville TN
37204

The Cherokee Five
& the Cussin' Tree

George Edward Spain

Ideas into Books®
WESTVIEW
Kingston Springs, Tennessee

Copyright © 2020 George Edward Spain

ISBN 978-1-62880-204-7

Ideas into Books®
W E S T V I E W
P.O. Box 605
Kingston Springs, TN 37082
www.publishedbywestview.com

All rights reserved, including the right to reproduction, storage, transmittal, or retrieval, in whole or in part in any form.

First edition, June 2020

Printed in the United States of America on acid free paper.

Dedicated to

Doug Wright — Billy Bob
Tommy Carter — TC
Joe Bush Miller — Bush
Martin McNamara — Double M
ME — GE

and to
my long time friend
Carolyn Wilson
1936-2019

Acknowledgements

Special thanks to Sandy Zeigler who prodded me to publish these tales and to Mary Catharine Nelson, my stalwart publisher.

Introduction

It was wonderful learning the glories of life: looking at the women's underwear ads in Sears, Roebuck catalogs, t-teeing our initials in the snow, telling dirty jokes, drinking Mr. Miller's liquor, shooting burning arrows in the sky and setting a field on fire, killing Nazis and Japs, running through the State Capitol, stealing our parents' cigarettes and cussing at the "Cussin' Tree" as we smoked them. Our days of summer were about as close to heaven as you can get.

Here we were, a band of five young boys whooping and laughing and running our way through WW II on Grandview Drive and Caldwell Lane in south Nashville: three Church of Christers and two Catholics. We were playmates, best boyhood friends, who could not have said it then — but I say it now — we loved each other.

Within each of the following stories is a golden nugget of truth.

Contents

We Were the Cherokee Five 1
Cry Havoc 7
The Cherokee Five Plus One 33
How We Helped Win WWII 49
Then Ends and Begins Again 69
Pony 71
Those Green Summer Hills 89
Ride to Glory 91
The Great Revival of 1953 101
The Sword In The Attic 105
Apaches 127
Kings X And Time out 151
Would You Give An Eye To See A...? 153
Halloween 1946 171
Ah! Summer begins, begins 179

IN THE BEGINNING

We Were the Cherokee Five

Other than millions and millions of people being killed in Europe, Asia, and Africa, we grew up in what we believed was a peaceful world where people knew their places and how they were supposed to behave; where whites and blacks, rich and poor, educated and uneducated, and Christians and heathens accepted their places in life and didn't make a fuss, or go out and march, and demonstrate. If they did, it didn't touch our lives.

As you read these stories you're going to hear, see, maybe even smell, my four boyhood friends and me and our world, a place and time a tad different, than the one we're living in now. Yet in many ways it wasn't so different from today's lives with all our lusts and loves and laughs and tears. Two of the stories, *The Cherokee Five* and *Cry Havoc*, are told about the same event, each one in its different way is super-dooper!

Looking back on The Cherokee Five, I can't help wondering why we were never caught and charged with delinquency, or why none of us ever became criminals. Surely God wasn't watching over us for our joys were mostly found in sins regularly cooked up in hell by the Devil for us. As Flip Wilson said, "The devil made me do it."

How could such good people as our parents have produced us? They taught us good manners — "Yes Mam, No Mam, Thank you, I'm sorry' — all the nice ways and words that showed we were 'raised right.' And we could act right and did when we were around grownups. But when they weren't — well — that's where these stories come from.

It also needs saying that all our parents likely had their own secrets. Getting old I've learned that it's as true of me as it was of my father who treated his family with so much affection, yet he was an episodic alcoholic involved in the numbers rackets and sold black market tires to his best customers during WW II. And was the best father I could have had. Though I don't know any hidden vices of my buddies' parents I'm sure they had some. If not, that's nice, but in a strange sort of way I'm a bit sorry for them — for my growing up was exciting and it's kept on that way.

I think that man tries to be better than he thinks he will be,
I think that that is his immortality, that he wants to be better, he wants
to be braver, he wants to be more honest than he thinks
he will be and sometimes he's not, but then suddenly
to his own astonishment he is.

William Faulkner

I don't remember if some of the stories I'm about to tell happened at the beginning, middle, or end of that glorious summer of 1946 when I got a whipping almost every week for something I did that was so wonderful I can still hear it, smell it, and feel every speck of it seventy-four years later.

*****

The Cherokee Five:

Billy Bob (12) The oldest of our group, our heavily freckled leader. Ruled over us with his fast fists.

TC (11) When it came to creating disgusting deformities he was the master with his eyelids turned inside out.

Bush (11) My best buddy, whose devout Catholic family—who drank all kinds of alcohol openly—saved me from many prejudices.

Double M (11) Living all the way over on the next street he was not quite a full member but he had the best climbing trees and a barn.

GE (10) I was the youngest, the chubbiest and the quickest to come up with ideas for devilment.

Cry Havoc

'Cry "Havoc!" and let slip the dogs of war.'
Mark Anthony
Act 3, Scene 1, Julius Caesar
William Shakespeare

It was July, 1946 and hot as hell — the kind of naked-sweat hot like the real hell where I knew I was going for stealing my grandmother's snuff to dip at the *Cussin' Tree* where I, who my gang called GE, and my buddies, Bush, TC, Double M and Billy Bob went to hide from our keepers, to smoke, talk ugly and look at women's lingerie pages in the *Sears and Roebuck* catalogues. I prayed to God that instead of me, He'd take my sister's mangy rat-terrier that was always hiking its leg up to pee on my leg.

Just twelve months before, the good old United States of America had beat hell out of the Krauts and Japs. And we'd helped win it for us by shooting down Nazi Stuka divebombers with our bows and arrows and b-b guns. I was ten; the others were eleven and twelve. Billy Bob was our leader.

But the Krauts and Japs weren't all gone; I'd discovered two who were hiding out in Nashville. And I'd found out where they were. We had three weeks to finish them off before we were to be sent back to the prisons our parents locked us up in what they called school for nine months every year, mine even incarcerated me for a couple of months every summer. Since I'd entered the first grade at David Lipscomb at age four I'd done a lot of hard time — which had hardened my genetic tendency for doing the devil's work.

But that summer I'd discovered a Kraut and Jap hiding out in the basement of the twelve-story Bennie Dillion building, the tallest building in Nashville and figured out what they were up to. I'd heard them whispering in the elevator when Bush and I were coming down from the top floor. We'd gone there to see how far down we could spit between the handrails in the stairwell. He'd beat me one spit. The elevator was crowded; mostly big bosomed, fat women. I needed a gas mask: I was being smothered by two huge breasts that smelled like talcum powder and, what I guessed was supposed to be fields of lilacs. Bush had disappeared somewhere beneath the dirigibled bottom that belonged to the breasts.

The Kraut and Jap were crammed into the corner behind us. Both were dressed in overalls to disguise themselves to look like workmen. I could catch snags of what they were saying, The big one, kept guttering, "Yah...Yah", the other — a little runt — hissed what sounded like, "Ah sooo...Ah sooo." Coming up for air, I glanced over my shoulder and saw a large man with a blonde, short, neat, Nazi haircut, and a little guy with slanted eyes and skin that looked jaundiced.

Then I heard bits of words that took my breath, they were mostly the Kraut's, "Parade...Fourth of July," and one that sounded like, "explosions" and the Jap giggled, "Ah sooo... HeeHeeHee...Boom, Boom."

O dear God in Heaven...they're goin' to kill us all before I can scream, **'The Kraut an Jap are goin' to Kill all of us on the 4th!'** I squatted to the floor. The woman with the battleship breasts hit me on the head with her purse and with a voice that cracked like a whip commanded, **"Young man get up off the floor and quit trying to look under women's skirts. Your mother would be ashamed of you."** And she hit me again.

Then, *Thank you Lord, You've probably saved my life,* the elevator door opened onto the first floor and everybody poured out, grimacing down at me as they passed. One old woman whose eyes looked strange stuck her tongue out and screeched, **"Prevert!"** I didn't know what she meant.

Only Bush and I remained in the elevator with the Kraut and Jap. They were standing behind us and couldn't get out. Bush was looking away from me like he didn't want anybody to know he knew me. We didn't move — I couldn't — I was praying so hard, *Please God don't let 'em see me...they'll torture me to get a confession...then it's into the furnace in tha basement...O God please!*

Suddenly, the Kraut bellowed in what was clearly an SS command, ***"VARKENS-NEUKER, GET OUT OF MIJN WAY!"*** And shoved me aside. I heard a whimper — mine — Bush's slumped body was trying to disappear.

They left the elevator. I crawled over and peaked around the side. Ah Sooo opened the door to the stairway and held it open for Yah who marched through and headed down the steps toward the basement with Ah Sooo right behind. I put my hands on the wall of the elevator and pulled myself up I was so weak I felt my blood had turned to water. I looked back at Bush; he'd shrunk to half his size. His eyes were stretched so wide they were about to bust out of his head; his mouth was open but nothing came out. "Damnit Bush, **GET UP**, let's see where they go." He straightened and followed me out as others began to push around us into the elevator; one well-dressed woman, with jingling things hanging from her ears, grimaced at us as she passed.

The elevator closed behind us. We were alone. I eased toward the stairwell door, ready to leap and run if the Kraut or Jap came out. Bush was glued to the back of my body. I turned the doorknob, eased the door open a sliver, and listened. Nothing. Not a sound. I pushed the door open wider and tiptoed in with Bush's shadow breathing on my neck. "Back up Bush, your breath stinks."

We went down half a flight of steps, stopped and listened. I could barely hear them. There was hissing and clanking. Then, faintly...

"Yah...Yah, It's almost time...is everything ready?"

'Ah sooo."

Then silence

"Bush, did you here that?"

"What?"

"They're ready."

"For what?"

"To launch an attack."

"Where?"

"Here in Nashville."

"When?"

"On the Fourth."

"I can't hear 'em, you sure they said that?"

"Damn right. You must be deaf from the measles."

"I never had 'em."

"Well then, they're stuffed with dirt…**Listen…they're gonna try to kill us all…we gotta get home!**"

By nightfall I'd gotten the other guys on the phone and next morning we were all at the Cussin' Tree where I filled them in on the Kraut and Jap's plot. I ended with, "Ya'll, you know what this means, we didn't finish 'em all off. We gotta get these last two before they bomb the parade, then we'll sure nuff be heroes an' they'll put our pictures on tha front page of tha papers."

"Damn right we will!" said Billy Bob. The others echo'd, "Damn right!'

You could see their eyes and movements speeding up with the righteousness of our calling to remove the last threat of evil to our nation.

"Ok, so how we gonna do it?" asked TC who was beginning to shift his feet back and forth like he was about to pee in his pants.

"We're gonna blow their asses outta that building!" They looked at me.

"How'n the Devil we gonna do that?" asked Double M.

"With an M-80."

"An M-80? Damn GE, that could blow tha whole building up...tha only thing bigger than an M-80 is dynamite."

"Naw it won't. Daddy got me some for tha Fourth an I've shot a couple off; if we drop it just right down tha stairwell it'll scare tha hell out of em an then, when they run out, TC can finish 'em off with arrows." TC was a humdinger with his bow. He could hit a gnat at fifty feet.

Everyone was silent, they waited for Billy Bob to speak, his jaw muscles were twitching into hardness as he turned and looked at us with his steely eyes that were saying, *'Let's get em.'*

"Men, prepare for war! Tha enemy is in our midst. We gotta eradicate them!" I didn't know what'n hell eradicate meant but there was an edge of a sword to his voice that sounded like a cold-blooded killer. I could see on Bush's, TC's And Double M's faces they didn't know what'n hell eradicate meant either but we all stood up side by side and began to chant **"Eradicate 'em, eradicate 'em, eradicate 'em..."** until Billy

Bob said, "OK, that's enough...GE give 'em tha plan."

I had it all worked out. "OK, here's what we're gonna do; all of you be at my house by 8:00 in tha mornin' an' Daddy'll drive us downtown to his car lot on Broadway when he goes to work. I've got two M-80's an' matches an' TC you bring your bow an' ask your Daddy if you can borrow his fly rod case; tell him you're takin' it to the Sportsman Store to see about tradin' it in for a new Fred Bear. Everybody wear your best runnin' shoes. Got it?" They nodded. "See you at 8:00."

We went home to prepare for war.

Next morning, we crammed ourselves into my father's 1945, powder blue, Cadillac with glistening spoke wheels. In Nashville Daddy was known as the "Cadillac Man" since he sold the best and drove the best and the fastest. During the war he could even get them for his best customers. I told him that TC had his bow in his father's fly rod case and was going to see about trading in for a new one and after that we were going to the

Rex Theatre to see the new Lash LaRue western at the Rex Theater. The Rex was tiny; it had about five seats on each side of a narrow aisle; it smelled like piss and the street bums who came to see cheap westerns for fifteen cents. Before we'd get our tickets we'd go down to the Arcade and get a bag of popcorn that was big enough to feed a family of seven for a week.

Of course I was lying to my father. I was beginning to discover that lying was a gift God had given me and doing it came easy. Later on, it became a great blessing for my writing.

When we left Broadway and climbed the slope on Seventh Avenue to Church Street we were right across from the Bennie Dillon Building. We cased it carefully from the outside; no police, no parents, no preachers, priests or teachers, no faces that looked like Krauts or Japs, no faces that might know us.

Once inside we would split up. Bush and I would take TC with his bow and rubber-tipped arrows to the third floor, which had corner windows in an empty room that opened out onto the two streets where people would have to flee from the building. Billy and Double M were to go to the sixth floor. Billy Bob's last command was, **"Synchronize your watches, we'll launch our attack at exactly O Ten A CLOCK."**

Double M asked, "What does synchronize mean? And O Ten A Clock don't sound quite how the military says time."

"Shut up Double M, let me do the thinking. **OK boys, over tha side...Let's take that hill!"**

As we charged through the first floor doors into the entrance we were invincible. We were storming Omaha Beach. We could not be vanquished. Our enemies would fall before us as we shouted, **"God bless America!"**

No one was in the side entrance lobby. I held my right hand up for every one to stop, put my left forefinger to my lips and eased the stairway door open to the basement — and listened. The others leaned forward.

Except for the sound of steam it was silent. Then, faintly, voices came from below, "HeeHeeHee...Ah sooo...Ah sooo." And as the last 'Ah sooo,' was hissed came the Kraut's voice; it was almost identical to Hitler's stridency in its mixture of German and English, it sounded like, "Ve vill conquer them, ve vill...**Seig Heil!**"

"**Men, man your stations!**"

We rushed upward.

Bush and I raised the windows as TC opened the case and methodically took four arrows out, laid them on the window sill, then strung the bow, fit an arrow onto the string, bent the bow all the way back — and waited. His eyes concentrated on the street below.

Billy Bob and Double M had gone on up the steps. I looked at my watch. Five minutes passed...six...seven...eight...

And then...**O my Lord**...**O my Lord**...and then, came an explosion, that sounded like most of half of Nashville had blown up; the sound traveled up, then down, then back up the stairwell. For a moment I couldn't hear. I hit the side of my head. Silence. I hit it again, and heard — screams and shouts and, just as I was about to run I glanced out the window and saw the Kraut and Jap come running out onto Seventh. From the corner of my eye Bush was standing like Robin Hood with his bow bent, taking aim, holding it...holding it...tracking his target then, **"TWANG!"** and — the arrow disappeared downward.

The Jap went to his knees grabbing his right thigh. And, in one smooth, continuous motion TC released a second arrow. Two long strides ahead of the Jap, the Kraut was running for his life when he suddenly reached back with both hands and shouted, **"GODVERDAME!,"** grabbed the back of his neck and pitched forward like a sack of horse turds. He was crawling toward the sidewalk when a second arrow bounced off his butt; for a second his face glanced back in terror and twisted in pain **"NEUKEN!,"** and crawled faster. Just as he was struggling to get to his feet the third arrow hit his butt in the exact same place and he let out a scream that didn't stop, **"NEUKEN, NEUKEN, NEUKEN!"** and, fell down on his knees and began praying, crying out words I couldn't understand. I guess they were some kind of words that were begging God to save him.

"Gotcha," declared TC.

I grabbed TC by the shirt collar, pulled him back from the window and hollered, "We gotta get out of here or we're gonna be strung up by our you know what's if they catch us."

He looked at me and grinned, "I did it...I got 'em...I got both 'em sons of bitches!" and then, he began to methodically put the bow back in the case, closed it, turned and we ran like hell was on fire behind us and raced out the door, down the steps to the first floor, turned right and went out the front onto Church.

The street was filled with people, police cars, fire trucks and ambulances. We ran across the street and ducked into the alley by the Paramount Theater from where we could watch for Billy Bob and Double M. As time passed we began to think they had been caught and were being tortured to confess who the other terrorists were that were helping them. Police came and went through the front and side doors. Every time the police came out we expected to see them dragging Billy Bob and Double M along in handcuffs and leg chains.

With all this excitement and running we got terribly thirsty and hungry. "Damn, I'm starving," groaned Bush. "Hell, they're probably dead by now, probably been tortured to death to tell who their fellow assassins were. Let's go get some Krystals and cokes and come back here and while we eat, GE you stay and keep an eye out for them."

"Yeah, that's a 'Bully' of an idea," said TC who was always quoting Theodore Roosevelt because his grandfather did. He was up on his feet with his fly case in hand and out on the sidewalk turning in the direction of Krystal. Bush tried to push ahead of him but was elbowed back.

"Wait up you guys, I'm comin too," I hollered.

We were not gone long. When we got back to the alley only a few gawkers with nothing else to do remained; the fire trucks and ambulances were gone, two police cars were still there: one on Church, the other on Seventh. TC and Bush sat down, leaning their backs against the brick wall, and began stuffing themselves, leaving me at my post to do all the watching. I took quick bites off my Krystals and stared at the building's windows and front door for signs that Billy Bob and Double M had survived.

As my mother used to say, "There was not a sign of hide nor hair of them."

We waited — One Hour.

— Two hours.

Not a sign of hide nor hair of them.

Bush and TC were asleep.

"Get up you guys." They didn't move. I kicked their shoes. "Come on get up!" They groaned and slowly got to their feet. "OK, keep behind me."

We crossed the street and went around the corner to the Seventh Avenue entrance. An officer was standing smack dab in front of the door

We waited.

Suddenly the moment came. The officer stepped away from the door to talk to a couple of giggling young women who wanted their photograph beside him.

We rushed inside and up the steps.

The building was quiet as a graveyard. We checked the hallways and restrooms as we went up to the sixth floor.

Nothing.

Then, there they were on, squnched down in the women's bathroom on the seventh floor. When I opened the restroom door and whispered their names, there came the weakened, tearful voice of Billy Bob from the third stall, *"Help...O dear God help me."*

TC's came from the same stall, "Hurry ya'll, he can't get his hands undone.

"He can't get his hands undone...what'n hell?" I asked.

"Their locked together around the door handle...he dun't look good."

"Can't yeh pry em apart?"

"I tried, but he started cryin' an cursin' an beg'n me to stop."

"Damnit GE, quit jabberin' an slide under an help TC pull my fingers off this damn thing!"

I slid under the stall and squeezed upward. TC looked scarder than I'd ever seen him. His back was pressed against the wall behind Billy Bob who was squatting on the commode; his dead white fingers and hands in a death grip on the door handle. He looked up at me — his face was pleading, but his voice still had some edge to it.

"Get back Double M...get back, an give GE some space to get em off, cause you ain't worth a damn at it."

I began to pry, starting with the little fingers, then working upward. But each time I'd pry the tip end up it would flip back down when I let it go and the next joint stayed fixed to the handle. The hands didn't budge.

Next, I gripped one arm and Double M gripped the other and we leaned back and jerked.

For a minute I thought he was dead. And then he whimpered like a baby, "Stop...stop. You're breaking my fingers,"

We stopped. We were sweating. Billy Bob's face was ashen.

"We need some grease to put on em," suggested Double M.

"Yea, but we ain't got any."

"How bout water?"

We began to spit on them. We spit til we were dry.

"That's not enough," said Double M.

We got him under his arms and heaved again.

He didn't make a sound. He was dead. This time I was sure. I could'nt look at him. "What are we gonna do with him Double M?"

"Whata yeh mean?"

"We've killed him."

"No we ain't"

I looked at Billy Bob again; his eyelids were flickering, he took a deep breath, "Damnit, ya'll are killin' me!"

We were so focused on the task we didn't pay any attention to him.

"I know what," said Double M.

"What?"

"Let's pee on 'em, the piss 'ul work its way down between the fingers an the warmth will loosen 'em up an' 'voila', they'll come loose.

Now and then Double M used one of the few French words his uncle Buford, who had fought in Belgium, France, and Germany had taught him; some he couldn't say around grown ups because his mother would have spanked him and sent him to bed without any supper and, worst of all, she wouldn't have let his uncle take him places and teach him things he needed to know, things like pissing on your hands which he had done at Bastogne to warm and loosen them up it was so cold.

When Billy Bob, heard "pee" on his hands his came wide open and he sat up the best he could, "Whatcha mean piss on my hands? I'll be double- dog damn if that's goin' to happen!"

"OK Billy Bob, OK, but the police are gonna come back in a bit, so it's either piss or jail." While Double M was saying this he had started unbuttoning his pants, "It's either piss or jail."

"OK, OK, but you just better only hit my hands an not pull my arms outa their sockets!"

"OK, we ain't gonna hurt you." we said.

In a second we both had our teeteers out and were pissing away.

Pulling on Billy Bob had torn a little skin off both his hands and when the piss hit them he let out a loud, **"DAMN THAT STINGS!"**

I had more pee in me so it took a bit longer before I tucked myself away and we got hold of Billy Bob's arms.

"OK, GE when I count three pull like hell...Ready?"

"Yeh."

"Three!"

Billy Bob let out a screech louder than an owl.

And came loose.

Bodies, arms, legs, and curses tumbled backward on top of one another.

Double M and I slowly disentangled ourselves, stood up and looked down at Billy Bob.

He lay in a fetal position beside the commode; not moving, not whimpering, not cursing.

"Well, we've killed him for sure this time," one of us said.

"Well we sure did," said the other.

We couldn't take our eyes off of him. It was like looking at the mummy in the State Museum. Dead forever.

And then, his eyelids twitched.

"O hell GE, he ain't dead, he's turned into a zombie." Double M was trying to get out the door but his hands were shaking so hard he couldn't open it.

Billy Bob sat up. Double M who was Catholic like Bush grabbed around my body and pulled me in front of him and began to pray, "Hail Mary, full of grace, the Lord is with thee...Hail Mary, full of grace, the Lord is with thee..."

"Damnit, Double M, shut that gobbledegook up, you all've probably broke my fingers an' bent em' back permanent forever...Damn, Damn, Damn!"

Billy Bob was back!

"OK," he said, "I'm takin over! Let's find tha rest of tha squad." As soon as we stepped out into the hallway we heard them laughing. They were in the stairwell—spitting. "Well I'll be damned, they're in there playin when they're supposed to lookin' for me!" He threw the door open so hard it slammed against the wall and scared the hell out of them; more so when they looked up and saw Billy Bob standin' there like he was going to hurt them someway bad. His jaw muscles were twitching. He was pulling on his fingers trying to stretch them then balling them up into a fist.

Billy Bob's cold-blooded killer voice returned, "OK, I'm takin over from here on...Get Your asses in gear, we're gettin' outta here, **NOW,** an' none of you'd better make a squeak, if you do your mother 'ul likely never see you tonight...We've completed our mission an' sure as hell, ya'll end up getting' some kind of medal an' most likely I'll get tha Medal Of Honor.

"We've done it again; we've saved tha good ole USA!"

*****

Next morning, on the front page of the *Tennessean* was this article:

Yesterday, at exactly 1:33 PM, there was a loud explosion inside the, twelve story Bennie Dillon Building at Church and Seventh. Pandemonium broke out: patients, families, doctors, nurses, and secretaries rushed from the building out onto the streets where a large crowd quickly gathered. In no time, the police and firemen surrounded and entered the building looking for injured and damage. None were found. It was soon determined that a large firecracker had been exploded in the stairwell. There were no signs of the culprit or culprits. Along with the explosion a rather bizarre incident occurred. The police found two men sitting on the sidewalk on the Seventh Ave. side. One said he could not walk. They were two maintenance men for the Bennie Dillon building: Mr. Ditmer Jurgen from Holland and Mr. Dominador Santos from the Philippines. Both claimed to have been struck by rubber-tipped arrows as they fled from the building. Mr. Santos gave two arrows to the investigating officers. Mr. Jurgen, who says he was hit three times, was taken to General Hospital for further examination but was released when it was determined his injuries were not severe. We have also learned from Chief Lester Jett that the building had been thoroughly searched and has been declared safe for occupancy and that all offices will reopen on Monday.

*****

Fearing death, we never spoke of that day again, not even at the Cussin' Tree.

THEN WE BECAME

The Cherokee Five Plus One

It was mid-July and God was warning us what hell was going to be like if we didn't change our ways. Not only was it hot as hell: but every evening all the lightning He ever made came down in jagged swords in the west. His answer to my prayer was deep rolling thunder like Nazi artillery which made us think the war wasn't really over even though all the grown ups said it had ended the year before. The five of us, being ten to twelve, had learned grown ups could lie just like we did — it was a hard lesson to learn when we figured out there was really no Santa Claus. I thought my best friend Bush would never stop blubbering.

I'd named us the "Cherokee Five." It took hold with the others because they admired my grandfather's great grandfather, James Vann, a half Scot, half Cherokee Chief who killed his enemies without mercy — bunches of them. He shot them, hung them, and burned one or two at the stake. He was the real thing, everything you'd want at least one of your ancestors to be. The others envied me for having him in my blood. Well they should have, for later in life it gave me excuses when I behaved abominably — "It's the Vann blood."

Since coming out of our mother's wombs all five of us believed in God but even more in the Devil. Billy Bob, T.C. and I were Church of Christers but poor Bush and Double M were Catholics which could only have come from an evil curse put on their families for they had to eat fish every Friday until they died. But I'll give them this, Catholics had one thing that beat the Church of Christ hands down — confessing their sinful ways to a priest and then doing, what they called "penance," which amounted to saying, "Hail Mary" thirty-three times and counting a bunch of black beads. When they finished they were home free — to begin again.

Now compare that to what Church of Christers had to do. In front of thousands, a sinner who, most everybody already knew the particular awfulness they had done, had to stand up in their pew during the "Invitation Song," and run the gauntlet down the aisle to the front pew scared so bad you almost wet your pants. I know, 'cause I did it once.

You ask, "Well, what did you do?" I'm not going to tell.

Every Sunday before Church or Mass all of us were put on the rack and tortured with ties tied so tight they cut off the blood flow to our brains. If you struggled the tie pulled tight as a noose. And then you were stuffed in a suit like you were a bag of potatoes, your hair was slicked back with water, the inside of your ears cleaned and swabbed and checked, and then, with a big smile, your mother would say, "Now don't you look sweet as an angel for Church." Gag! It was absolutely horrible.

Have you ever seen the black openings of a double barrel twelve-gauge shotgun? That's what our preacher, Brother Black's eyes looked like. He dearly loved the Old Testament God who obliterated Egyptians and cities and entire peoples including little children, mothers and old people. Of course, as he explained, it was all for the good so mankind could be taught a lesson: that He was all powerful and those who went against Him had to suffer in order that He might show to those who remained that He loved them.

I swear to you, whenever his voice hardened about God's destruction of tons of sinners Brother Black looked straight at me no matter where I was sitting; and I swear he was grinning. That night I'd pray like the devil for mercy and promise to change my bad ways. But then, to be totally truthful, there was another side to all of it, for there was a part of me, a big part, that enjoyed his horror stories: all those lions and fire, jawbones of asses, seas of water drowning chariots, horses and all those hundreds of thousands of Egyptians. What I saw in my mind was better than Cecil B. DeMille's, *The Ten Commandments*.

Before television, before videogames, before smart phones, before growing up and having to make a living, we had — except for two torture chambers, school and church — all the time in the world to imagine and create. And we did. In fact we were Olympic champions in imagining and creating. In those days of perpetual summer, education and religion were like gnats we swatted away

We did our imagining and creative planning at the cussin' tree. Now, before going on with what we came up with I've got to add in another guy who was visiting for a week with his aunt who lived down the street. He was a year older than me and another Church of Christer. We'd known each other from being in the same Sunday school class since we were little. His first and second names were so awful you wondered what his parents had against him. Soon as I'd taken him to the cussin' tree to meet the others we gave him a new name as his real ones made us gag. We called him CAB, the initials of his name.

This day it was TCs time to bring the cigarettes. He took — stole, I should say — a pack of his father's Lucky Strikes. As we passed it around and shook one out it came to CAB. He passed it onto Double M without taking one. We were about to light up when Billy Bob said, "Hold up ya'll. Why'n hell didn't you take one CAB?"

"Cause my Mama told me she'd whip the daylights outta me if she ever caught me smoking. An she really hurts when she whips."

With that the others began, "Chick...Chick...Chick," and then everyone began to chime in -

"Come on CAB, one of these 'ul put hair on your chest."

"Yah, an it'll be worth a beatin'."

"Yah, an we won't tell 'cause all of us 'ul get a beatin' too."

"Yah...Yah...an yah you don't wanta be a chicken the rest of your life."

"Yah, an if ya smoke it, we'll make ya an honorary member of tha Cherokee Five."

His hand shook as he reached out and took the cigarette.

"OK now, put it in your mouth."

He put it in his mouth. Bush struck a match and held it up to the end.

And CAB took a deep draw and...

...Bent over and began to cough his lungs out. For a moment I thought he might vomit.

We all began laughing and slapping him on the back.

He staggered, straightened, and slowly eased down to the ground with his back against the cussin' tree, took another draw, stretched his legs out and smiled.

Then came the bombshell. One hand at a time CAB reached into his right pocket, one hand at a time, pulled something out gripped in each hand like he was holding pieces of gold or diamonds. His eyes glittered. We pushed up close and stared down at his hands. He said nothing. His eyes lit his face.

"Whatcha got there, CAB?" asked Double M as he reached toward CAB's right hand.

CAB pulled it back, "Guess," he said.

"Well I'll be damn, open your hand or I will," said Billy Bob.

Slowly the fingers began to unfold and there, in each of CAB's palms, was an M-80 firecracker. Years later they were outlawed. An M-80 was the next thing to a stick of dynamite. We all stepped back. Double M whimpered. "Well I'll be damn," followed by a chorus of "Damns."

As the final damn came CAB asked, "Do any of ya wanta hold one?" There was a long hesitation then I said, "Sure."

My open hand was shaking when I held it out — it all seemed in slow motion, He dropped it into mine. It did not explode. My hand was still there. It had quit shaking. I was alive. I held it like a baby. "Well guys, whata we gonna blow up?" I asked.

After coughing out a few more 'Damns' the ideas came spewing out:

"Let's blow up the school."

"No, No, No...let's blow up the church."

"Let's blow up...uh...uh...everything."

"You dumb-bells, we'd all end up in prison and hell."

'Well, how 'bout one of those statues at the capitol?"

This went on and on until we had run out of ideas and were about to fight, then Billy Bob said, "OK, OK, everybody SHUT UP! Here's what we're gonna do."

Stone silent we waited.

"We're gonna test it on that old rotten, hollow stump out in tha field...Let's go."

We ducked under the wild hackberry hedge that surrounded our gathering place beneath the cussin' tree and took off through the sedge and briars to the stump.

And there it was — three feet tall. It had once been a giant. But, as with all living things, the giant had fallen and was crumbling back into the earth.

CAB was grinning like a possum eating briars. Two M-80s had made him one of us — The Cherokee Five.

"OK, CAB, put it in."

"Hey you guys, lets put some rocks around it," said Double M whose uncle blew up old buildings.

We picked up rocks and stuffed them around the M-80.

The explosion made quail flush, rabbits run and crows lift from their perches and fly from the surrounding trees. Up on the hill, across the field, I heard a man shout, "What'n hell was that?"

Rocks had shot up and out, one hit Bush on his elbow. He grabbed it and bent forward, "Damn that hurt like hell!" The rest of us ducked and rolled laughing on the ground. We knew either God or the Devil had sent us a gift. Now, how were we going to give it the honor it deserved?

And, as in that opening verse of the old gospel hymn, 'a voice comes ringing o'er the restless waves,' "Let's drop it down tha stairwell at tha Bennie Dillon Buildin'."

It was CAB's. He'd heard us brag about spitting down the stairwell and how your voice echoed when you yelled.

"Well I'll be damn," said Billy Bob.

After four more 'I'll be damns,' CAB said, "How 'bout tomorrow?"

'Damn, Yes!' we sang together.

The next day, Saturday, was perfect. Most downtown offices were closed. We told our parents we were going to see Lon Chaney's most recent vampire movie. Each of us had a dollar for the movie, three Krystals, a chocolate bar, drink, bag of popcorn, and bus fare to town and home — .90 cents.

'House of Dracula' almost made me wet my pants. Dracula must have sucked out a gallon or two of blood before it ended. It was great! When we walked out onto the street, into the light, all of us had mustard on our mouths and chins except for CAB, whose mother had preached into him that cleanliness was next to Godliness.

But now the time had come to hit the beach and take the enemy by storm. No one spoke. Our eyes were fixed, mouths grim; focused on our objective we moved as a team up the street, shoppers separating as we pushed through.

And then, suddenly, there it was, rearing up before us — the Bennie Dillon Building — twelve stories high. For a moment we did not move as we looked up in awe. "Alright men, follow me," Billy Bob commanded as he opened the side door. We followed him into a small elevator lobby. No one else was there. Except for doctor's offices and a few office workers the building was empty. CAB pushed the button. The door opened immediately. A sickening grin was on his face as he made a sweeping gesture for us to enter. We elbowed one another into the landing craft. The door closed behind us. We were headed for Omaha Beach.

Except for Billy Bob and CAB the rest of us didn't look well. In the back of my head a tiny voice was whispering, "This ain't gonna turn out well." When CAB pushed the button for the twelfth floor and the elevator jerked I knew one of us was going to vomit before we got to the top floor. Next there came a gagging sound. The others edged away from me.

"You better not vomit GE," barked our commanding officer.

"Ever things ok ole buddy," soothed CAB.

Floor lights flashed, flashed, flashed. We moved closer and closer to hitting the beach. I'd stopped gagging and was ready as soon as the door fell open. The elevator shuddered to a stop. The light was on for the twelfth floor. We were there.

The plan was this: to avoid attracting attention the six of us would walk quietly out, turn left around the corner to the stairwell door which Double M would open and one by one we would file through and stand without speaking around the railing of the stairwell. Six inches separated the handrail all the way down to the bottom floor. CAB would get the M-80 out, hold it over the handrail space, TC would light it and when it was spewing CAB would drop it and we'd all run like hell and if we split up we were to meet in the alley across Church street.

The time had come. It was going like clockwork. CAB'S hand was steady. He was grinning. TC struck the wooden match. The flame flared. TC held it under the fuse. The fuse spewed. CAB held it and held it and grinned like a madman. *Drop the damn thing... he wants to kill us all.* Then, he let it fall. We all ran.

Stumbling, shoving, cursing, we began to run in different directions. CAB and Billy Bob ran into the hall toward the men's room. TC and Double M took off down the stars. I went around the corner and got in front of the elevator. I don't know what happened to Bush.

For a moment there was no sound. *Well I'll be damn, it didn't explode.*

BAARRROOOOMMMMMmmmmm.....mm mm......mmm

The explosion's thundering sound traveled up and down the stairwell; it's echo went on and on and on. Suddenly, doors in the hallway were flung open, patients, secretaries, nurses and doctors came pouring out shouting, **"What was that? Is the building falling? Do we need to get out?"** There were whimpers. A baby cried.

I took up the shout, **"What was that?"** Then, thank the dear lord, the elevator opened and a sobbing women and I pushed in among some who were already in the car. Fear stamped their faces, 'What was that?' I pushed my head back between two big breasts — a brief comfort.

The door opened on the ground floor and we ran through the lobby out onto the street where a crowd was gathering, everyone was shouting, 'What was that?' From nearby came sirens, then flashing blue and red lights, police cars, ambulances and fire trucks.

Air, sweet, sweet air. I gulped it in. My legs were like spaghetti but I could still walk. I looked down as three policemen ran past me into the building. I couldn't see any of the other guys. *O lord, they've got them in there pressed up against the wall putting handcuffs on them* I crossed over Church, turned, passed two stores, and ducked in the alley where we were supposed to meet up. Gasping for air, TC and Double M came in a moment later; then Billy Bob. "Where's Bush?"

"How'n hell should I know? I left him behind. He's slow as molasses."

And Bush appeared covered in dust. He smelled like cleaning stuff. "Were'n hell did you go?" asked Billy Bob

"In a cleaning closet. I thought I was gonna smother to death."

"Did ya see CAB?"

"Un un."

We all grew silent. *Where was CAB? Did they have him? Were they torturing him to get him to confess and give them our names? Would we all go to jail or be shot?*

"I'm hungry," whined Double M.

"So am I," I said.

"Anybody got any money?" asked Billy Bob.

Between us we had enough money for two Krystals, one order of fries and one large Coke. Billy Bob got the money and sent me to get it.

When I came back to the alley there was CAB. He'd just hidden in a stall of a women's restroom when frightened women started pouring in. "I had my feet up on each side of the door and was gripping the handle so tight I almost couldn't unlock my fingers after they all left — Hey GE give me one of those burgers."

After we finished arguing over how we would share the food and eaten, it was time to go home. What a glorious day! One of the best for the Cherokee Five — and for Plus One.

How We Helped Win WWII

WWII—more than God—cast its shadow around my world and the worlds of my four boyhood friends while barely touching the edge of our day-to-day lives. Not one of our fathers was in the service. Not one of our mothers was a "Rosie The Riveter." The heavy droning of bombers, the thundering of artillery and the screams of wounded and dying were oceans away. Fire and falling walls, the stench of blood and decay, the gaunt faces of hunger, the gaping mouths and crushed bodies were the lives of other boys. Our war, the war we saw, was in *Life* and *Movietone* newsreels, in newspapers and the happy faces of soldiers and sailors on our streets; and in the occasional jeeps and trucks on our streets and the planes and gliders that flew over us; and there were ration stamps, Victory Gardens and Uncle Sam posters; and there was Mr. Wright who lived two houses down from us; he was our volunteer Air Raid Warden who wore a helmet and sometimes let us walk with him when he checked on "blackout nights" to be sure curtains and shutters were drawn and closed so no lights would guide German or Jap bombers to bomb our homes. The shadow of war was so far away it never nightmared our sleep. It was not real. Our world was summertime and Christmas and laughter and the adventures of our play.

Finally the war ended.

But not for us.

*****

All of my uncles had come home safely from the Army, Navy and Air Force. Nobody I knew had been killed. Though I've never breathed a breath of this to anyone until now, inside my head I was more than slightly disappointed that not one relative, even if only a second, third, or fourth cousin had given his life on the field of battle, or in the air, or on the high-seas and then, after several rounds of rifle fire and bugle-notes, had been buried with full military honors at sea or in a national cemetery. It was an early lesson in life; that you don't always get everything you dream about.

Johnny Banner, the only brother of Betty Banner—the prettiest girl on our street or, for that matter, on every street for miles around—had returned home from Europe. He'd been all over France and Germany reporting for the Stars and Stripes. It's still hard to believe; he came home loaded with all kinds of neat Nazi-German war stuff, which he gave to my buddies and me. My buddies being: Bush and TC, who each got a German army raincoat that snapped together to make a two man pup tent, and Billy Bob who got a mess-kit, and Double M who got an ammunition belt. But, I think it was because he knew I was madly in love with his sister—even though she was twelve and two years older than me—that he gave me the absolutely, positively, most perfectly, splendid thing an American boy could get: a German helmet with a bullet hole smack dab in middle of the front and, to add to its splendor, there was what looked like real blood stains inside around the hole.

In my mind, what Johnny Banner did ranked him right up there with Tom Mix, the Green Hornet and Superman as one of my heroes. And Betty? Well she was the first and only love of my young heart, a heart that—except for mothers and aunts who didn't count—had not yet known a real woman, nor the love that comes from loving a real woman.

Then there was TC's uncle. We all wished he had been ours. Whether he was trying to or not with his clipped mustache, dimpled chin and wide grin he looked a lot like Clark Gable except he didn't have Gable's big ears. He was a real "Flying Tiger" Ace in China where he had flown P-40s with a shark's face and big teeth painted on their front. He knocked down fourteen Jap Zeroes from the sky. You'd think that killing Japs the way he did that the furthest thing from his mind would have been a young nephew back in Tennessee. I met him only once and then only for a few minutes. He tousled my hair and I felt like I had received a blessing. He must have been another special kind of man like Johnny Banner for he brought back something for TC that was extra special nice but; nowhere near my German helmet with German blood around the bullet hole.

When he gave TC a Chinese warrior's bow and a quiver full of arrows with sharp iron arrowheads, I thought TC's eyes were going to pop out of his head. Inside of the bow, near the handle, was a Zen saying written in Chinese. Though it didn't look like real writing to me his uncle could read the stuff. First, he read it in Chinese, which sounded a lot like metal clanging together. Then, he read it in American, *"In the case of archery, the hitter and the hit are no longer the opposing objects, but one reality."* That made absolutely no sense: to me nor to any of the others. No one asked, "What's that mean?" We just squinted our eyes seriously at it and nodded like we knew.

TC was an absolute archery fiend. He was good at it. All five of us had bows but his was a "Bear" a real Fred Bear bow. As soon as he got it he wanted to show it off. It was the real stuff. He took it to the backyard to try it out. I couldn't even bend it. Billy Bob's arms shook so hard he let go and the bow string smacked him on his forearm so hard he let out a, "Dad gum it!" and almost swore but caught himself because TC's mother was hanging out clothes. The arrows had long feathers. You could kill a deer with them, or a Jap, or a Nazi. The bows the rest of us had were either homemade or cheap things made for shooting at paper targets. They could make a dog yelp but that was about all.

*****

We were at the Cussin' Tree. We'd just finished the Camels Bush had stolen from his sister's hiding place. It was mid-morning. A breezy day. We stood there wishing we had more Camels. And thinking. Trying to come up with the day's adventure. Then, out of the blue, Double M, who was not known for coming up with masterful plots and brainy plans, said, "Let's paint our kites like Stuka dive bombers an' shoot the Huns from the sky...Lets use our bows an' arrows and BB guns like artillery and machine guns." He called the Germans "Huns" because that's what his grandfather who had fought in WWI called them.

Still no one spoke. Our brains were turning what he said over, slowly at first, then quickly, it began to take shape and there it was—Double M's blazing idea shooting straight up into the sky.

With a slight hint of admiration, Billy Bob said, "Well, I'll be damned Double M! I didn't even think you had a brain. Let's get those Nazis."

The rest of us followed up with our, 'I'll be damns.'

"Let's kill those Krauts!" chimed TC.

"Shoot their Heinies from the sky!" Bush and I said together and burst out laughing. We loved the word "Heinie."

We knew we had the day by the tail. And to top it off, the wind was picking up.

"Well, I'll be damned!" Billy Bob repeated.

"That's a bully of an idea," Bush said, whose father was always quoting Theodore Roosevelt.

"A real bully of an idea," I echoed. Next to mine, Bush's father was my favorite of my friends' fathers.

"Ok, everybody go get your bows an' arrows an' BB guns. I'll bring my kite. Who else has got one?" asked Billy Bob.

"I have," said Double M, raising his hand.

"Me too," chimed TC.

"An' me too," I said

"And I'll bring some paint an' brushes from my dad's shop so we can paint 'em. I'll see ya'll back here. Everybody hurry like hell," said Billy Bob, as he bent down and crawled through the secret passageway we had cut in the hedge that surrounded our refuge from our parents.

"Alright men," Billy Bob commanded, "Get your weapons an' hurry back to your battle stations. **Double time it!**"

*****

The summer before, we had sworn to our parents that we would only shoot our bows in our backyards when an adult was present. We made lots of promises to our parents during those years, but the "backyard promise" we halfway meant after TC almost killed me.

It started out as a pleasant afternoon in my backyard. My parents were away. We decided to play *Chicken*. The idea was: we would lie on our backs in the grass and not move and TC would shoot a steel-tipped arrow straight up in the air; as the arrow returned anyone who jumped or rolled away was a "Chicken." And, anyone who didn't move was either: a hero, a wounded hero, or a dead hero. Three times the arrow shot skyward. Three times we were all Chicken.

Then, on the fourth, I didn't move. I squeezed my eyes shut and said a quick prayer, *Dear God, my mother loves me and she loves you too. Save me!* There was a thud. *The arrow has struck me in the heart. I have only one more breath, only one more thought left in me, 'Mama!* There was a scream far back in my head, but it wouldn't come out. Why would my mouth not scream? I am dead. That's why. I am dead*!*

Then came a scream. A real scream.

"EEEEEEEEEE!!!"

But, it wasn't my scream leaving my head. It was Cornelia's, our maid's scream, **"Oh, my dear Lord Jesus! EEEEEEEEEE!!!"**

I could hear her pounding feet, her heavy breathing coming closer and closer. I still hadn't opened my eyes. I couldn't. I was afraid of what I would see sticking out of me.

The last tremor of the scream and the last deep gasp for air was ten inches above my face. Then, strong hands gripped me by the shoulders and I was lifted from the ground and hugged so tightly against Cornelia's big bosoms I thought I was going to die, not from an arrow, but from bosom suffocation.

The only time Cornelia ever whipped me was on that day as she was dragging me by my hand back to the house; all the while declaring, "You done scared me ta death...You done scared me ta death...You get in that house now an' you ain't goin' out ag'in 'til yo mama an' daddy gets back." Then came the three blows; they were more like the pats you give someone you love who needs comforting.

But that night, when my parents returned, my mother's laying on of hands was not a patting. And, as always, she honored that perverse pact of our mothers and called the others to report our most recent act of savagery. So, once again, before we could have our suppers, each of us had to add another promise to our long list of promises, "I swear to never ever again..."

*****

We were out of breath when we got back with our weapons to the Cussin' Tree. God had heard our prayers. We had gotten away with our bows and BB guns and kites without being seen.

With his bow and quiver over his shoulders, Billy Bob stooped low as he came through the hedge that surrounded the Cussin' Tree. He carried a large, well made, bright-red kite, two cans of paint and a dried-out paintbrush gripped between his teeth.

We were waiting there for him with three kites, four BB guns and five bows. TC had wrapped cloth around the heads of two of his arrows. Sticking above his back pocket I could see the spout of a lighter fluid can. The time for all out war had come. We were going to save our nation and the good people of the world. But first—

"Holy Jerusalem, Billy Bob, where'd you get that?" asked Bush pointing at the red kite. "It's a beaut!"

"Un-huh," said Double M, without his lips moving.

Billy Bob: put the cans and brush on the ground and held the kite up, turning it slowly for us to admire and long for.

"Mama got her for me for my being so good. Today, it'll be flown by Red Baron the Second, son of the legendary Red Baron, Germany's greatest WW I ace."

"Did you say you got it for being good?" asked Double M.

"Man, you pulled one over on your mama." I said.

We all laughed.

Billy Bob's eyes got hard and his fists doubled up. We shut up. "OK, let's get 'em painted and in the air," he hissed.

He opened the cans. One contained a putrid green paint; the other black. Three kites lay beside the buckets.

Most Nazi planes were painted that exact same putrid green; with black crosses on their wings. Billy Bob went to work. In no time the kites were painted. They were ready to lift from the earth and rain death and destruction on civilization and the people we were sworn to defend.

With weapons and Stukas in hand we went to the field beyond the hedge. It was covered with weeds and scrub-brush, once part of a long-gone, green golf course. It was sided by three streets that, except for mornings and afternoons, had little traffic. Only a few houses looked down through a screen of trees onto the field. The battle we were about to unleash would not be interrupted by the real enemy—grown ups.

"Bush, you and GE fly the planes and the rest of us 'ul do the shootin'"

"Damn, Billy Bob, I wanta shoot to," I said.

"Well, somebody's gotta fly the planes...tell you what, ya'll do the flyin' an' I've got two extra cigarettes I'll give you."

"Now?"

"No, not now dummy, after the battle."

"Well, how 'bout a half one now?"

"Damnit, GE, you'll get it when it's over. Now, get the planes up in the air."

Their motors roaring, the Stukas hurtled down the airfield and soared into the air. The blitz-krieg had begun. Explosion after explosion came nearer and nearer. Smoke rose in the distance. We could hear them approaching. Billy Bob shouted, **"Are you ready men?"** And then—there they were against the blue sky, the black crosses like the markings of death. They rolled from the sky, one after another, shrieking downward, their machine guns flashing fire like sparklers. **"Give 'em hell!"**

Pffit-Pffit-Pffit, the bullets whipped past our ears, striking all around us, kicking up dust, cutting through small saplings, ricocheting off rocks; the noise of the diving planes and machine guns was deafening. **"Fire-fire-fire!"** They opened up with their rifles. They had no effect. The roar of the planes was deafening. Everyone was yelling.

The dive-bombers rose from their first strafing run then, they turned and came straight back.

Bush pointed at the lead Stuka, **"Get 'im! Get 'im!"** Side-by-side, they fired as fast as they could cock them and pull the triggers. It zoomed right over their heads. We could see the bullets striking but nothing happened. It rose with the others and began to make another turn.

"Load the artillery...we got to get those Krauts!"

They laid the BB guns down, picked up the bows and quickly strung arrows.

"Here they come again," Double M **hollered.**

The first one zipped over untouched. The second one got by. But, as the third Stuka started to stoop, TC fired and, suddenly, the bomber came to a halt in mid-air; the arrow struck its cross-frame breaking it in two. It shuddered to a stop and then, shaking back-and-forth, fell to the earth.

"Well, I'll be damned!" said Billy Bob.

And the rest of us followed up with our, I'll be damns.

They reloaded. And waited.

TC brought the second one down with an artillery shell through the tail.

We began to chant, **"TC, TC, TC!"**

But the last Stuka was piloted by Nazi ace Red Baron the Second. It came roaring down, dodging and twisting, its machine guns firing and firing, spewing death and destruction. As it zoomed over Red Baron the Second leaned out of the cockpit and shot a finger at his enemies.

"Shoot the son-of-a-bitch, shoot the son-of-a-bitch TC!" shouted Billy Bob as he shot a finger back at the bright red dive-bomber as it made its turn; the roar of the engines became a high-pitched scream as it bore down with guns spitting fire.

At that moment, out of the corner of my eye, I saw a red flash. I turned. Six feet away stood TC. He looked like Robin Hood. His left arm straight out, his hand gripping the bow's handle; his right arm crooked back, his fingers pulling the taunt bowstring all the way to its maximum, the arrow's feathers touching his fingers, the front of the arrow's shaft resting on the top of his left hand, the cloth covered arrow-head extended a few inches beyond the front of the bow—the cloth was engulfed in flame. TC's face was set in stone, as grim as death; his unblinking eyes fixed on the shrieking Stuka. He held...and held...and held...until I thought he had been hit and was standing there dead.

And then...and then...his fingers twitched and released the string, the arrow shot forward, the flames on its head swept backward as bits of burning-cloth flickered in the air. Like a fiery rocket, the thin arrow's trajectory streaked upward in a diagonal line that struck the plane, breaking it into pieces of fire—but that was not the end—the arrow streaked onward, higher and higher, until it came to the end of its arch where its flame curved downward and downward, falling into dry brush and sedge.

Oh, how glorious it was—it burst into a conflagration of fire; the leaping flames and smoke rising higher and higher, with the wind spreading it quickly across the field toward the tree line and the street beyond.

No one spoke or moved.

Then, Bush spoke, "Well, I'll be damn!"

"Well, I'll be a double-dog damn!" said Billy Bob.

"Damn...damn...damn...damn!" I couldn't stop saying, "Damn."

TC's eyes stretched wide like he was seeing the end of the world.

And, maybe he was, for in the very next moment people came running out of their houses. Women were standing with their hands over their mouths. Men were running toward the fire with rakes and shovels. There was shouting and a few screams and many curses.

I'd heard preachers preach the world would end in fire; that everything was going to be burnt to a crisp. Maybe this was it. Maybe we were seeing it start. Maybe we had started it. Nobody seemed to notice us. For the moment we pyromaniacs were invisible. People and dogs were running back and forth, a cat was stepped on, there was yowling and howling and, over and over, a crusty old voice tried its best to shout, "Call the fire department...Call the fire department...Call the police...Call everybody!"

Suddenly, between the all the pandemonium and clamor there was a split-second of silence and, in that split-second, there was a high-pitched whimper, "I've got to hide." I looked to my side. TC was pirouetting in a tight circle, his face was the face of terror, "Oh my Lord, Oh my Lord they're gonna hang me for sure!"

Above his whimpering; above the yelling and barking, and screeching; above the flames and billowing smoke; above the weeping and gnashing of teeth; from far away, there came the strident sirens of fire engines and police cars racing nearer and nearer.

And then they arrived.

*****

It is the anticipation of death that most often is more feared than when death actually comes. So it was with us. The horrors of torture to extract our confessions, the horrors of coming punishments, the horrors of eternal damnation in hell; these horrors pressed our eyes open in the darkness of our nights. Yes, we would one day be found out and, if on that day, we were not killed outright we would likely be put to the rack. But, it needs to be said that—

No matter our pain.

No matter our tears.

No matter our penance.

We were the heroes who shot down Red Baron the Second.

We were the heroes who helped win WW II.

We were the heroes who helped save the earth.

To this day it is glorious.

Then Ends and Begins Again

On that side of summer's beginning
When children laugh while playing
Their fabulous ways toward death
And griefs are fixed to tears
Though never wiped away
Heaven hangs on a high hill
Where winds whirl faith away
Before the last cock crows
And time runs down into a hollow
Of the heart until it is filled
                              then ends.

Within the heat of winter's spinning
Golden nets are set for flying unicorns
On whose horns shibboleths
Of fire forked light appear
In words that melt away
All jacks of frost until
The tears of spring lose their way
From out the eye and flow
Into a flood where flowers grow
And time which is never stilled
                              begins again.

Pony

The glob of spit shot—out—out—out—and still out until, finally, it curved downward and hit with a—**SPLAT**—two feet beyond a battlefield strewn with spittle. Like a warrior-king, Billy Bob leaned triumphantly back on his elbows. His was the regal smile of one who has again assured his superiority by right of arms.

It was summertime. The five of us and an assortment of dogs were taking up most of the sidewalk in front of Hutcherson's Pharmacy and Landon's Hardware Store. Our stage. Here, like strolling contortionists, we regularly performed our bad habits. There was always a passing audience of grownups to be impressed with our ability to spit, or to witness the extraordinary dexterity required when you tightly pressed a thumb against one nostril—and loudly blew your nose.

When we ran out of spit and mucus, we would saunter into Landon's. Landon's! Military arsenal and weapons' supplier to the summer soldier: B-B guns, pocket knives, cap pistols, bows and arrows, sling shots, pea shooters, and all the materials you needed to make that piece de resistance of summer warfare—rubber guns. Rubber guns fired loops cut from automobile inner tubes. The loops were knotted and stretched tight from the end of the wooden barrel to the clothespin trigger held to the back handle with a band of rubber. Few things in life are more satisfying than hearing the solid whack of knotted rubber hitting the bareback of an enemy playmate. A scream of pain makes it sublime. For the rest of the day, the success of your crafty ambush was there for all to see—a fiery, red whelp. Had we set our ambitions toward cold-blooded mayhem we would have ranked right up there with Attila and Bonnie and Clyde. As it was, our dogs and cats and younger brothers and sisters constantly watched us out of the corners of their eyes, creating in their minds ugly sounds and pictures—the rat-a-tat-tat of machine guns riddling criminals full of holes—like Swiss cheese.

Since, the dogs and shoppers were bedazzled by our spitting they deserved an encore. "Let's do our deformities," said T C and immediately began turning his eyelids inside out. Once turned, they could stay that way for hours. Then, a silly, pompous grin would spread all across his face. He knew he had the rest of us hands down when it came to looking deformed. The rest of us weren't even in the same league. Bush could only bend his fingers back to the wrist and my best was your basic lower leg, out of the joint, walk. But T C was really horrible. You could see it in the startled faces of old ladies who walked hurriedly around us to get in the stores. When you looked at T C dead on, and saw those blood-red strips of raw flesh above the whites of his eyes, it was just about the most sickening thing you can imagine. Today, he wasn't grinning. He had an intense, fixed stare that seemed totally unaware of the rest of us. When I saw both of his eyelids suddenly flip down, I realized he was experiencing something powerful. I followed his gaze. And then, I saw her...

Standing like a golden statue in the summer sun, was a pony standing alone on the school playground across the street. She was stunning — a glowing, palomino pony with a flaxen mane and tail — she was the most beautiful thing I had ever seen. A real, live pony; symbol, nay, the very embodiment of our play: Robin Hood, Mountain Men, Lee, Stonewall Jackson, Tom Mix, Cowboys and Indians, warfare of every sort—and through it all we rode straight and strong, striking our enemies down, right and left and on—to victory! High upon that pony's back we would be able to look down on all the rest of humanity — for they would be beneath us.

Glitters of light surrounded the pony. Double M, who liked to read stories about old-timey days, said the glitter looked just like the halo he had seen in a picture of King Arthur's charger. "Gnats, just a bunch of gnats," Billy Bob pronounced. Billy Bob ruled over our gang with the divine right of quick muscles and preferred to dictate the day's visions. "She looks more like something Forrest would have ridden when he whupped up on them damn Yankees." We played Civil War a lot and, of course he always commanded the winning side—the Rebs. He was either: Lee, Jackson, or Forrest, and sometimes all three in one battle. He said any dummy could see he had to be the commanding general, since he was the only one who had a Confederate general's hat. It was a cheap, felt thing with a Rhode Island Red chicken feather stuck in the band. He liked to call the feather a plume. While I'll have to admit that the hat had style, the truth is that not one of those generals went around with a plume sticking out of his hat. And if he had, it wouldn't have been an old beat-up Rhode Island Red chicken feather.

The pony had not moved. She was totally alone. She was lost! She was ours for the catching, and ours for the riding. And as we were learning the ways of the world, our minds were already calculating that she represented hard, cold cash on the hoof. Such gentle beauty had to be some sweet child's dearest possession. We were assured that, loving his child as he did, some rich daddy would offer a reward, would give us money, for our good deed. Since she had no halter, Billy Bob told us to go into Landon's and buy some rope. He would keep his eye on the pony. In a flash, we were in and out with the rope. And still the pony was there, as real and as beautiful as ever.

Frantically, we set to work on a lasso. The rope was twenty-feet of cotton nightmare. Knot tying is an art, and the only one we had down pat was the standard, impossible to untie except with a sharp knife blade, shoelace knot. All ten hands started twisting, looping and knotting at the same time. It looked like we were trying to come up with the getting burned by rude rope yanks. That gave way to bad name-calling, then to shoving. We were right on the verge of a free for all when we stumbled onto it. It looked like something that was half-lasso and half hangman's-noose. I know this, if I'd been either a horse or a horse thief, I wouldn't have wanted that thing around my neck. But it was going to have to do, or we were going to end up killing each other.

Then, Billy Bob spoke, his words were chilling, "Double M, since you know so much about horses and chargers and stuff, how about you putting that rope around her neck—we'll back you up."

Well now, when it finally gets down to the actual fitting of your imaginings with your realities, they don't always square at the edges. Movies about cowboys and playing cowboys are one thing, but walking right up to a wild stallion and trying to put a rope around its neck, that's another. A sickly look was concentrating itself on Double-M's face. I could see his fingers trying to squeeze up and hide in his hands. He began to sag all over, as pure fear turned all his bones and muscles to mush. Billy Bob said, "Double M, you ain't goin' chicken on us now are you?" There it was. Chicken! Better to have bubonic plague, leprosy, or only one leg than to be called, "Chicken." It was a condemnation worse than death, for it marked you for the rest of your natural-born life. Once you were labeled "Chicken" your only options were suicide or moving to another town.

Double M took the rope and, like a man going to his own hanging, struck a death-march pace, as we crossed the street. As slow as he was moving, the rest of us were slower. He was our friend, and we wanted him to have plenty of room to run if he needed it. It was like we were in a slow motion film, a classic scene: the King of the Wild Horses is finally cornered; the relentless sun beats down; the five dust-covered cowboys close in; the brave roper moves cautiously up to the horse's head. If the stallion goes for anyone, it will be him; the time of truth has come! The film slows, then stops on a drama filled scene of the Old West: At the end of a sun-bleached ravine, five sweat-stained cowboys stand, lean and hard, before a great, wild stallion; one figure holds a lasso right at the point of passing it over and around the stallion's wide-flaired nostrils and chiseled head. And then it happened...

The pony flicked her tail, stomped at a horsefly, curled her lips back from her teeth and gave a long-drawn, high-pitched whinny. Double M screamed, dropped the rope and ran smack dab into Bush. As we ran, everyone was hollering. I could hear a strange whimpering coming from my throat, and Billy Bob kept saying, "Dear God, save me...dear God save me."

When we were safely back inside Landon's, and in the back of the store, we turned to see if the frenzied beast was coming straight on through the glass window to kill us all. Double M was so scared he was stuttering, "D-D-Did you see th-those teeth? They c-could have r-r-ripped my arm off my b-b-body!"

Sucking hard for air, Bush gasped, "Those hoofs could have kicked our brains out."

Since the plate glass was holding firm. Billy Bob said, "T C, Go up there and see what that thing is doing."

T C said firmly, "Ununh, I ain't going by myself. You gotta come with me!"

There was a pause, and then Billy Bob said, "O K everybody, let's go!"

With muscles tensed tight in anticipation of an instant need to leap to safety we eased up to the window and looked out. The pony had not moved. She stood there splendid in the sun. For a moment, no one spoke. Then, Double M, his voice back to normal, whispered, "Hell, she's just a pony. I'm goin' to get her." With shoulders squared, he went right out the door without looking back. By the time the rest of us were across the street, he had the rope around her neck and she was nuzzling his hand.

For the remainder of the day, we led one another around the schoolyard, with one and sometimes two, of us sitting upon her broad back. Now and then, we would stop to let her rest and graze. As she munched the green grass we lay around her, admiring her gentleness and all of her loveliness. Her golden coat was soft as silk and when, for a moment, she raised her head to gaze far away, the peacefulness in her eyes gave us joy. It was a day filled with sun—and it was heaven!

But a new problem arose as the sun began to set. Now that we had her, where were we going to put her? T C said, "How "bout Brother Black's?" Brother Black was a Church of Christ preacher who taught at Lipscomb where Billy Bob, T C and I were students. He had a field nearby where he kept horses. It was a double-barreled idea. Being that Brother Black, God, Billy Bob, T C and I were so closely tied together it would give Brother Black a chance to do a good deed for everyone. And, as Bush and Double M were Catholics, it would be further proof that the rest of us were on the winning side. Not that we really needed it, since their having to eat fish every Friday, for eternity, was plenty of evidence that God didn't look kindly upon them.

When we got to Brother Black's I volunteered to handle the negotiations. Since the Lord is on the side of the righteous, I wanted the lead position in showing Bush and Double M the error of their ways. The congregation waited behind me in the yard as I offered Brother Black the opportunity to strike a blow for the Lord. And then, with a big smile on his face, that Man of God looked down upon us, and in his best preacher-voice, said, "A dollar a day boys, a dollar a day, that's what I charge everybody, and to be fair that's what I'll have to charge you, a dollar a day."

What did he say? Did he say a dollar? A dollar a day? He's supposed to say, "God love you, you fine young fellows, bring that beautiful creature of the Lord's right on in here. Bless you for giving me this chance to do good. I won't charge you a cent. For it is written, 'It is more blessed to give than to receive.' Praise the Lord!" What in hell did he just say? A dollar a day? Hell, we ain't got a dollar a week among us. Hellsfireanddamnation! What he just said was, "No!"

Looking down at my feet, muttering as I stumbled away, "Thanks...we'll see...maybe, thanks a lot." *Hellsfireanddamnation, hellsfireanddamnation.* As I passed Bush and Double M, I hissed, "If either one of you laugh, or say anything, I'll bust you in the nose."

Pony in tow, we returned to the schoolyard, to think.

As we set there in the evening shadows, I was sure I heard a snicker and saw some quick smirks pass between Bush and Double M. *Damn the fairness of greedy preachers—now what are we going to do.*

Finally, Billy Bob spoke up, "Well, we gotta do something and do it quick. The only other place is Mr. Naked's."

We called him, "Mr. Naked," because he was an artist who specialized in painting naked women. And if that wasn't bad enough, he had two, gosh-awful, gigantic dogs that could kill and eat a grizzly. He lived in an old, run-down house surrounded by vines and hedges. Just thinking about it started my left eye to twitching. My future prospects suddenly took on a bleakness. If I saw one of those naked women, I'd probably go blind. And if those beasts saw me, I was going to disappear forever down their throats. But we had to risk it. Mr. Naked was our last chance.

I'd just about had all the excitement I could stand for one day. This time, I wasn't volunteering for anything. The fact is, nobody was. When we pushed our way through those dog-fanged hedges, it was going to be all for one and one for all. *Come on pony.*

We stood before the great, walled hedge that surrounded Mr. Naked's house. It was a Dracula film: the wild, forsaken forest of Transylvania., filled with vampires, werewolves and packs of man-devouring dogs. The night was dark as a wolf's mouth. Bush whispered through his clenched teeth, "You remember those women vampires who slept in those boxes at Dracula's castle...you don't suppose Mr. Naked and those women..."

"Shut up, Bush!" tongue chopped Billy Bob.

I could tell my hearing was sharpening as we crept through the hedges. Listening for the flap—flap—flap of descending wings. *Can vampires hear you heart booming? Damnit, who keeps stepping on the limbs? They* cracked like dry bones. It was the pony. *I may have to kill her. Better her than me.*

Between the rustle and crackle of our footsteps, came a strange, almost imperceptible voice, "Dear Mary Mother of God forgive me, for I have sinned..."

Then another voice, this one near hysteria, "O' Jesus, I think I smell blood!"

"Damnit Bush, shut up!" Billy Bob's voice struggled against a scream.

We were out, and into the yard. In front of us reared a large, ivy-covered, stone house — the castle of Count Dracula. No one moved, our eyes froze on the iron-hinged front door.

The pony whinnied loudly and pawed the ground.

There before us was the maw of the beast. Light flickered through the door's small windows onto a dragon-headed knocker. The dragon's eyes moved with the light.

I heard my voice praying aloud, in unison with Bush and Double M, "Dear Mary Mother of God forgive me for I have sinned...Dear Mary Mother of God...

All I could think of was my throat. When that door opened, how was I going to keep whatever that thing was inside away from my throat? I searched my pockets for a weapon. Nothing. For the want of a cross, or some garlic, or a mirror, or a good sharp stake, I was about to be sucked dry.

Listen! "Click"...a lock turning. *O' my Lord, O' my Lord.* The door handle turned. With the rusty, strident, creaking of a coffin lid, the door slowly—ever so slowly—opened.

Standing in the doorway, outlined by the flickering light, was a tall, silent man; his face shadowed.

O' Lord, O' Lord. Children shouldn't have to die this way. Way down, deep inside of me, I felt the last scream of my life beginning to form. *O'Lord, here he...he...he comes.*

"Hello, boys. Can I help you?"

Count Dracula slyly requesting to fang our throats.

We stood there silent, like five stone statues.

"What's wrong? Has a cat got your tongues?"

Dracula the jokester.

He stepped toward us. But—it was just a normal step forward. Not a soaring leap that went straight to my throat. And his voice — it was normal. Not one of those hisses that turn into the last roaring howl you ever hear. It was just a plain, ole' everyday voice.

With wide-stretched eyes, we examined him. No wings. No cape. No death-white skin. No burning eyes. NO FANGS! Before our eyes, Count Dracula dissolved... disappeared.

And became...Mr. Naked.

"Whatcha got thah, a pony?" he asked.

"Yes sir, Mr. Nak...yes sir, she sure is!" said Bush.

You could see Mr Naked's eyes smiling as he admired her. "She's a beauty. Well boys, I'm guessin y'all might be needin sum help...Y'all are all noddin, 'Yes.' So I'm goin to guess y'all might need a place for that pony to stay. Right?"

The stars were out as we started home. Once, we stopped to hear the pony whinnying to us through the darkness. Mr. Naked had put her in his field. Then he had taken us into his barn where he fixed an old bridle and saddle for us to use when we rode her. She could stay there until we found her owner. And got our reward. When we asked what he would charge, he just laughed and said, "Boys, I probably ought to be payin y'all for lettin me keep such a splendid creature." He didn't want a thing. Not a thing. It was free!

As we walked on through that summer night, my mind kept going over and over everything that had happened to us that day. Somehow I knew something important had occurred, something that I could not yet put into words. But later on, way later on, it came to me—*things ain't always the way they appear to be.*

Those Green Summer Hills

Take my hand little boy
For together we must go
To those green summer hills
Where foxes laugh with joy

What golden glories we shall see
In that ancient hollowed land
For fairies on bumpy toadstools
Will dance with you and me

Knightly you will sit astride
A whistling tree horned stag
Your young heart filled with shouting
Now knowing the world has lied

For its blind eyes can only see
Things that are cold and real
Never feeling the warmth of dreams
That live in you and me

Ride to Glory

Billy Bob was literally eaten up with freckles. In certain kinds of light, his skin looked like he had some gosh-awful tropical disease. A thousand more, give or take a couple of hundred, and they would all have run together, turning him into one five-foot tall, skinny freckle. Then we'd likely ended up calling him "Nig," because he'd been permanently browned all over. Of course, calling him "Nig" would have made him fiercer than he was prone to be. For my sake, since Billy Bob was older and tougher than me, it probably saved my life by his not being a total freckle.

T C, Bush, and Double M made up the rest of our gang. Since Double M lived all the way over on the next street, he wasn't quite a full member. Our acceptance of him was helped considerably by his yard having the best climbing trees and an old barn that made a first class clubhouse and a fort when we had BB battles with the Cullum gang who all lived on the other side of Lealand Lane.

Double M and Bush were Catholics, which meant they ate a lot of fish. I've always felt that Fridays must have been hell on them. Maybe I shouldn't admit it, but I got a perverse type of pleasure when I ate cheeseburgers in front of them on Fridays, which I tried to do with regularity. Admit it, we all like having some solid, here and now proof, that we bet on the right horse when it comes to religion. Any kid will tell you that eating fish every Friday for the rest of your life is not even close to being in the money when it comes to cheeseburgers. It's a wonder they hung with it. If it had been me, I'd have joined another church, just to get the cheeseburgers.

Back then, in the summertime, kids turned out ideas faster than those Old Testament types begat children. When you haven't got television or air-conditioning, and your mama is committed to teaching you the American Work Ethic, it tends to influence creativeness in such ways as getting out of your house without being seen. Those of us that made it, gathered at the "Cussin' Tree."

The Cussin' Tree was a big, old mock orange tree that grew green, bumpy, soft-ball size mock oranges which dripped white sticky stuff when you stuck holes in them. They were hard and heavy and hurt like hell when you used them as hand-grenades. The tree was hidden in a place like Robin Hood might have had in Sherwood Forest. It's where we went to smoke and talk ugly. And it's where Billy Bob came up with the idea of turning our Red Rider wagons into soapbox racers and riding them through a wall of fire. Democratic type government wasn't Billy Bob's ambition when he was hot on some new and overpowering idea. At those times, his prepubescent squeak ruled over us like a Henry the Eighth bellow, even when we were questioning his judgment on things like walls of fire.

By the time we'd finished the cigarettes that Bush had confiscated from his daddy and pumped ourselves up with some fresh dirty talk, we had Billy Bob's idea roughed out into a plan. I'm telling you, in those days kids were whizzes when it came to creating. If we'd set our minds on better mousetraps, all of us would be rich men today.

Come the next day, we'd replaced the beds of our Red Riders with racing bodies made from wooden crates. Tied to the front wheel axels were guide ropes that turned them quicker than power steering. Needless to say, Billy Bob's had extra "horse-power," that is, an extension on the back for one of us to kneel on while we pushed.

His idea had come from a Movietone film that showed a stunt man smashing his car through a burning barn then, leaping out with his hands clasped high above his head while the crowd roared. As he acted out the leaping, hand-clasping part, I saw a semi-wild, excited look grow on Billy Bob's face, which caused me to tense up. I'd seen it before and had a flash back to the previous winter when I fell through the ice into Mrs. Foy's goldfish pond. On that day, he had turned us all into north-woods trappers. And now, here he was with that same fast-eyed look, telling us all about the glories of riding through a wall of fire.

Double M's street was perfect for setting walls on fire. It had a steep hill no traffic and best of all you couldn't see the bottom of the hill from anybody's house. It took awhile for us to drag a pile of cardboard boxes all the way from the back of Landon's Hardware Store to Double M's street. Billy Bob supervised the wall building. After a lot of adjusting to meet his specifications, it was impressive looking. It was four feet deep, eight feet high, and twelve feet wide. From a distance it looked like it would stop a tank.

By now, Billy Bob's movements were starting to get quick all over, like you get when you've just got to take a leak and your surroundings won't allow it. To tell the truth, I was picking up speed too. My muscles were getting jerky and my vision sharper. Now, I was seeing the beauty of it all. That great wall of roaring red, yellow and white flames rising to heaven, and me and Billy Bob riding through it to safety on the other side, where the cheers of the crowds were waiting for us to leap out with our hands clasped high in the air — as HEROES!

No one was going to push Billy Bob's racer but me. For today we were bound for glory.

We waited at the top of the hill; he, forward, in the driver's seat, legs squeezed down inside the wooden body, knuckles white with gripping the guide ropes; and me, kneeling on the back, one foot on the ground, one leg bent like a taunt bow-string, waiting to shoot toward our target. We waited, our eyes fixed on Bush, "Lighter of the Flame." He lit his newspaper torch and carefully laid the fire around the base of the wall. His movements, the first wisps of flame and smoke, all seemed unreal—slow—silent—sinister, like some ancient preparation for sacrifice. All sound was suspended as I listened for the command. I waited, and then it came—**"GO!"**

Muscles, bones, nerves, blood, flesh, all that was me released in one mighty heave, with such force that, for an instant, the racer's front wheels lifted from the ground, and then—we rocketed down the hill. Traveling at a velocity heretofore unknown by a Red Rider, our racer sped down-down-down, with wheels and wind whirling, as though we must lift from the earth into flight. We were a flash of light, rushing toward Billy Bob's fiery vision, which zoomed upward to strike us. Suddenly, for a final split-second, before my face, there was the roaring, burning, smothering wall of flame. My last thought was a flash image of a black, burned to a crisp, chicken-liver—Me! And then we hit, and were inside, all the fire God had ever made!

AIR—AIR—cool, cool AIR, free of fire, clean of smoke, quiet, sweet tasting—I was out, on the other side, safe and uncharred! I could hear a great, massed cheering from the wonder-struck crowds, and through it all, someone screaming my name. It was Billy Bob. He was on fire! From the top of the wall a single, small box had fallen, flaming, into his lap. He was trapped in the racer and screaming something awful, **"Get it off—get it off—get it off—get it off!"** With his attention seriously diverted, the racer zigzagged down the street, went into a spin, jumped a ditch and overturned. Dust, wisps of smoke, black flakes, and terrible language rose and spread around the wreckage. I was thrown clear.

T C, Bush and Double M rushed to the racer and dragged Billy Bob out and began rolling him in the dirt. I crawled toward them and slowly climbed up my legs onto my feet. We helped him stand and began to do our best to separate the dirt and gravel and black bits of charred cardboard from his flesh. He seemed to be totally unappreciative of our efforts, for between groans and whimpers, he'd flail one of us, then another, with the worst cussin' I'd ever heard. But we stuck steady to our task, we all knew there would be hell to pay if Billy Bob went home and his mama looked at him and he didn't look right. For all of our mamas were sworn to some unwritten, but binding, maternal pact of perversity to telephone each other whenever they knew, or even suspicioned that we had been up to no good. For they knew us, they knew that we had a righteous obligation to share with one another, the joys of our sins.

All and all, Billy Bob began looking better, especially after we had spit on our hands and cleaned his face. Double M kept brushing hard, with some leaves, on a big black spot on his t-shirt, until he was rudely pushed away. We stood back to observe our handiwork.

Everyone had hope on his face, especially Billy Bob. Like an artist seeking the slightest flaw on a finished portrait, we looked him up and down.

Nobody moved or spoke. The very silence suggested something dreadful. I looked at T C, Double M and Bush. Their eyes were stretched big-wide, and the skin on their faces had gone white, loose and scary. I got sudden, queasy, sick feeling, like a knife was twisting in the pit of my stomach. I looked again at Billy Bob, and there before me was the awful truth of our fiery ride.

Billy Bob's eyebrows were burned plumb off his face.

The Great Revival of 1953

*Dedicated to the 1953
Graduate Saints and Sinners
Of David Lipscomb High School*

I do not remember much, nor remember very well,
But this I know for truth and this I'll truly tell,
Every year in high school chapel,
There was held a Great Revival.
A preacher came and preached of sin
And fire, that sinners burned forever in.
It scared the you know what out of me,
As I think it did you, for I still see
Us all hunkered deep down in our seats
Trying to hide, while the preacher entreats
Us to, "Turn from Satan's way!
Come, come now; be saved this very day!"
Then with his piercing eye, he held me long,
And sang, and sang, and sang, the invitation song:

"Almost persuaded, harvest is past!
Almost persuaded, doom comes at last!
Almost cannot avail; almost is but to fail,
Sad, sad, that bitter wail — almost but lost!"

O Lord, I almost died of fright,
If *doom* did not strike me then, I knew it would that night.
I prayed, "Feet rise up and walk! Dear Lord, do not let them fail.
I promise, I swear, I hear that bitter, *bitter wail.*
Feet, damn you, move — and preacher keep on singing.
I'll come forward, if my feet will get to springing."
Then it happened, there went one of you, then two, then three and four,
Then more, and more, and more.
A host of teenage sinners went rushing down the aisle.
All their feet were working, and their faces all did smile.
My time was running out, with fervor I did pray,
But still my feet of stone did stay, and stay, and stay.

"Sad, sad that bitter wail — almost but lost."

"Lost...lost...lost," echoed clearly, finally...
and was gone.
Then silence, but for a whimper, that from
my mouth was drawn.
I prayed, "Great God Almighty, don't let that
song end there.
I promise I'm *persuaded,* but my feet won't
work, I swear!"
His answer to my prayer came quickly,
"Perchance,
Doth thou not remember all thy sneaking
'round to dance?"

The moral of this story is: Feet can lead you
straight to hell.
So, since then, to warn others, I tell my
terrible tale.
For what I've told you is the truth you see.
It happened to me, and it happened to thee,
thou Class of '53.

The Sword In The Attic

It was 1946. The war was over. It was summer in the land of the free. School was out, the sun was shining, and not one of us — not even me — had to go to summer school. As a reward, the Lord had sent us a gift; a new street was being built a half a mile from our homes. Bulldozers were already digging up the earth and somewhere in all that dirt; hidden treasures were waiting for us — us, being Bush, TC, Billy Bob, Double M and, me. Billy Bob, our leader, was twelve. He was the oldest. I was ten and the youngest.

The day was hotter than hell; you could swim in the humid air. None of our houses had air-conditioning; as soon as we could escape from our mothers we were gone, sometimes a whole day.

We gathered with our bikes in Billy Bob's back yard. Except for our shorts, we were naked. If not for being reported to our parents by do-gooder old ladies we would have gone naked as soon as we were out of sight of our houses.

Billy Bob's freckles were growing by the hundreds everyday the sun was shining and that was every day. Though I never breathed it aloud, I thought he looked like a colored man with some kind of gosh awful jungle disease. Double M and Bush were Catholics, which I figured was the reason their skins burned so easy. TC and I were the only ones with nice tans, me because I had some Indian blood, I don't know where TC's came from.

The new street was next to a big field where Brother Black kept horses. The summer before, Brother Black, a preacher and teacher at the Church of Christ school TC, Billy Bob and I attended had tried to beat us out of a dollar a day to keep a lost pony we'd found. All of our allowances together didn't make a dollar a day. As we walked away with the pony TC had whispered, "Scrooge." I whispered back, "He's *a tight-fisted old crap-head.*" Double M and Bush had smirks on their faces, seeing it was a blow for the side of the Catholics.

When we got to where the bulldozers had been digging we spread out and began to circle, like five sharp-eyed buzzards searching the up-turned earth for a dead rabbit, or dog, or better yet a cat. Our anticipation was probably better than anything we were likely going to find on the ground half covered with dirt. Hopeful anticipation is one of the things that helps you get up in the morning, if you don't have it, then you might as well roll over and go back to sleep. Or die.

One of the best things about living in the South, are all the dead people in the ground, they are everywhere: dead Indians, dead soldiers and just plain old dead people. Now and then, some lucky kid or archeologist will hit the jackpot; better than finding bones of dead people is finding bones of a prehistoric beast, especially something really big like a saber tooth tiger, or a giant bear, or a mastodon. Finding one of these would sure as anything get your picture in the paper and turn your playmates green with envy.

My dream was to find a stone-box grave with a complete Indian skeleton and a lot of gold jewelry; or a rusty bayonet with dried blood on it or a rifle barrel, even a Minnie ball; anything that had killed a Yankee. It would have been better than making straight

A's all year long and having a string of gold stars by your name. Finding a stone-box grave that hadn't been messed up by a dozier or a stupid grownup was the kind of thing that created such excitement that it almost made you wet your shorts or start a shoving match to see who got first bids on what was inside.

It was Saturday. No one was working. We had all the dug up earth to ourselves. The only others were a bunch of sparrows: scratching and pecking. We spread out, peering and sniffing at the ground. Occasionally, someone would shout and we'd run to them; our anticipations leaping us across the stones and clods to reach the shouter and to — nothing but an old tennis shoe or an Orange Crush bottle. I thought Billy Bob was going to hit Double M with a rock when Double M hollered because a bee had stung him. Billy Bob had little sympathy for us when we were in pain. "You sissy, spit on it and quit whining," was all the compassion and medical treatment Double M was going to get.

We'd been there about an hour, getting dirtier and dirtier, and tireder and thirstier by the minute, when all of a sudden, Bush gave a shout and enough "Damns" it made us know we'd better come running, "DAMN... DOUBLE DAMN! Ya'll look what I found! DAMNATION! DAMNATION!"

We stood around him in a circle and looked down. Six inches beyond our toes we could see the top of two broad stones. In various tones, we all echoed, "DAMNATION!" as we looked down at the top of what we were certain was a stone box grave. We had seen pictures of them in books and read in newspapers about people finding them but none of us had ever seen one in real life, much less found one.

The two slabs were clearly outlined beneath a thin covering of dirt. We waited for Billy Bob's orders. He was our leader because of his fast fists, which all of us had felt at one time or another.

Finally he spoke, "Well I'll be damn!"

We all nodded.

"Well, you guys quit standin there, get down an clean it off."

On our hands and knees we worked swiftly as though he had a bullwhip cocked above us and was ready to flay our naked backs. With a quick stirring of dust up into our eyes and nostrils, it was done.

"OK, OK, get back an let me do tha liftin so nothin goes wrong."

We stood up and took a couple of steps back and watched.

He squatted at the far end of the largest stone, reached out, crooked his fingers in the crack between the two stones, took a deep breath and began to stand, pulling the stone upward. His eyes and cheeks bulged; the places where he wasn't freckled turned red and he made a strange sound, like something was boiling inside his mouth. I thought his head was going to explode and splatter all over us.

Then it happened...the stone slipped from his hands and he fell backwards into the dirt.

We watched as it fell in slow motion — down — down — down. For a second, there was silence. No one breathed. No birds sang. The clouds did not move. The heat waves stopped rising.

The end of the world will sound like the sound that was made as the stone crashed back into the grave. There was a sharp cracking of bones and pottery, and the startled flapping of sparrow's wings as they burst upward and, above these, were our cries to God for mercy.

The dust blinded us. A little more and we would have smothered to death. No one moved, not even to help Billy Bob to his feet. No one spoke. We were struck dumb. All we could feel was a dreadful fear. We were frozen in a black and white photograph of people long dead.

"Well, who'n hell's goin to help me up."

Bush and T.C. pulled Billy Bob to his feet.

The dust was still so thick we couldn't see into the grave.

We waited.

And waited.

Finally, the air cleared. We stepped forward and peered down into the grave. What we saw was so far beyond disbelief no word has yet been created for it. The only thing that could have done more damage to the skeleton and pottery would have been six sticks of dynamite. All that remained was dust and the crumbs of the skeleton and pottery.

There was total silence. I think Billy Bob could see inside our heads. What he saw wasn't pretty. If he had spoken we would have killed him right then and there and stuffed his body into the grave, filled it in with dirt and rocks, smoothed it over on top. And then we would have: made a pact to never tell anyone, dusted ourselves off, gotten on our bikes, and gone home for lunch.

All we got were a few teeth and finger bones. I drilled holes in mine and made a necklace, I still wear sometimes on Halloween.

Ten minutes later we were at Bush's. We were starving. Mr. And Mrs. Miller, his parents, were gone for the day. Before I go on, I should explain that the world opened up to us when any of our parents were gone from home for a good part of the day. It was like going to Treasure Island. We searched our parentless houses better than the F.B.I. could have. Attics, basements, refrigerators, closets, under beds and pretty much anything closed that wasn't chained and padlocked was ours to find, to look into, to touch, to eat and even drink — and more, much more. We saw things we were not supposed to see, some we did not understand; we discovered relatives we had not known existed, some beautiful, some who looked like gangsters; and we learned of good things and bad things that brought smiles, sniggers and silence.

In the Miller's kitchen we turned into locusts. We drank all the milk, ate a whole loaf of bread, a jar of peanut butter, a jar of grape jelly and finished off all the cookies in the cookie jar. Then we went to the basement to the den. Bush flipped the lights on. What a den it was: with its large stone fireplace and pine paneled walls covered with photographs. The chairs and couch were covered with big cushions. But what made it the most special den I had ever seen was the bar and bar stools in the corner. On the wall, behind the bar, were three shelves filled with bottle after bottle of scotch, gin, vodka, bourbon, brandy, sherry and stuff I'd never heard of. The rows of gleaming glasses, their sparking reflections of light and the different colors of liquor, the varied shapes of bottles and labels, and stacks of glasses, was the next thing to any decorated Christmas tree I had ever seen. We couldn't take our eyes off of it.

Before anyone else made a sound, Bush said, "Ya wanta drink?"

Bush's family, the Millers, were genetically Catholic; which leads into the world of theology, a world where people lose their tempers easily and tend to get a lot of satisfaction out of shortcomings in those who believe differently than they do.

A good example is what I knew about Catholics:

1) They were condemned to eat fish every Friday for eternity.

2) They baptized babies by sprinkling water on their heads instead of shoving them totally underwater.

3) They had to sit in little closets and tell awful things about themselves and then a priest they couldn't even see would give them a lot of tiring stuff to do and say.

4) They had to do what they were told by the Pope who couldn't even speak good English, if at all, and wore a long robe instead of a suit and tie, like grown preachers should. Also, he wanted to take over the United States.

5) In school the nuns beat hell out of boys knuckles and palms.

6) They liked to drink and dance and gamble and have lots of children.

7) When they died they might have to hang around in a strange place for a long time before they ended up in heaven or hell.

8) They had a secret men's club called the Knights of Columbus where they took an oath to kill all kinds of people, most especially Masons. My father was a Mason.

When I'd say these things — except the part about killing — to Bush and Double M, they'd start getting offended and try to argue with me but nothing they said held any water, since I had heard the truth direct from the mouths of preachers and teachers.

I never showed Bush or Double M my authentic copy of the oath members of the

Knights of Columbus had to take. It had been passed out at school. It was long and went on and on until it finally reached the really good part:

"I do further promise and declare that I will, when opportunity presents, make and wage relentless war, secretly and openly against all heretics, Protestants and Masons...I will secretly use the poison cup, the strangulation cord, the steel of the poniard, or the leaden bullet...That I will provide myself with arms and ammunition that I may be in readiness when the word is passed, or I am commanded to defend the church either as an individual or with the militia of the Pope...

"In testimony hereof, I take this most holy and Blessed Sacrament of the Eucharist and witness the same further with my name written with the point of this dagger dipped in my own blood and seal in the face of this Holy Sacrament."

Well there it was in black and white. The first time I read it, it scared me so bad I dreamed that night about Mr. Miller strangling my father with a green and gold cord. I never showed the oath to anyone, especially my parents; I kept it hidden in the bottom of the cardboard box that held my comic books. I think I was afraid if my parents saw it, especially my father, it would somehow make it come true and would result in him being poisoned, or strangled, or run through with a dagger.

And it was going to be done by Mr. Miller. He was one of them. He was a member of the Knights of Columbus. The year before I was given the copy of the oath, Mr. Miller had taken Bush and me with him to the Knights of Columbus white, two-story building; right up the steps and in the front door and then through another door that opened into a high-ceilinged room, the size of a basketball court. He spoke to everybody and they spoke to him. They all seemed to be friends. They all called him "Johnny."

My eyes stretched as wide as they could go. The room, they called, 'The Hall', was a wonder to behold: slot machines, pinball machines, roulette tables, card tables and crap tables were everywhere. On the walls were paintings of men wearing dark blue robes and feathered hats, several with swords. Above the paintings, flagpoles slanted outward, some with American flags; others were gold and blue with green crosses on them. From the rafters, hung blue banners with gold lettering, many with the symbol of an ax head, sword and what looked like an anchor. At the far end, above the fireplace, were two crossed swords with silver blades and golden handles. Through an open door, I could see a dimly lit room with a bar and tables where men were drinking and laughing. But what made me really stop and stare: were two priests: one shooting dice, the other spinning a roulette wheel.

I remember little else, not even how long we were there. The strangeness of it scared me a little and I moved closer to Mr. Miller; yet there was a part of me, a large part of me, thrilled by it all.

Mr. Miller loved beer — Miller beer. He traveled all across middle Tennessee as a newspaper distributor. In the summer, he often took Bush and me with him. Every day, at lunchtime, he would take us to the best place, in whatever town we were in, that served good hamburgers, french fries and ice-cold beer. He always drank draft beer in a mug bigger than a soup bowl. Sitting across from him, I could hardly take my eyes off the white foam above the amber beer and the icy skim on the mug. It looked almost as good as a chocolate milkshake. When he drank, it made a white streak above his upper lip like a mustache, and when he salted it the foam rose like magic. He was a good man who liked to: tease me, laugh, and tousle my hair. He and Mrs. Miller and all their family were always kind; treating me as one of them. It was from them and from my parents, I eventually learned that: kindness can be greater than a lie and that, sometimes, kindness is even greater than religion. But that day had not yet come when I was ten years old.

"Well, do ya'll wanta drink?"

The words had barely gotten out of Bush's mouth the second time when we all shouted, "YES!"

"OK," he said, "Wait a minute." He ran from the room and up the steps and was back in an instant with an empty coke bottle filled with water and a funnel and towel. "I'll be tha bartender an do tha mixin, since it's my liquor an my bar."

With that, he turned and took down every open bottle. There were seven of them. Next, he got a tall glass and poured maybe four or five thimble fulls from each bottle into the glass. After the seventh bottle, he put the funnel in its mouth and replaced the exact amount taken out with water, put the top back on, wiped the bottle off, shook it a little and placed it back in its exact place on the shelf. He repeated this seven times; totally concentrated on his concoction, he never looked up; never said a word. It was like watching a movie of a great scientist in his laboratory turning out a cure for Billy Bob's jungle disease. We were in awe. I knew of no Church of Christ boy who had anywhere near this kind of genius. He was so good at it, it made think he had done it before.

After the last bottle was back on the shelf, he took a spoon from under the bar and briskly stirred everything together. He held the glass close to his eyes. When it was mixed to his satisfaction he looked up and said, "What'll we call it?

Billy Bob said, "How bout 'Witches' Brew'," which didn't have any imagination at all.

"Or 'Vampire Blood'," said T.C. who, still wet his bed after seeing a Bela Lugosi or Lon Chaney movie.

"Or, how bout 'Seven Farts to tha Wind', said Double M who had a thing about saying farts, and was always trying to work the word in no matter how inappropriate it was.

The night before I'd been to the movies with my parents. We'd seen a John Wayne war film that had left me feeling patriotic on the inside, "No you guys, they ain't any good. Since we just beat the hell out of the Germans an Japs lets call it the, 'Victory Drink'."

The others squnched their noses up and turned their thumbs down.

Then, with finality, Bush spoke, "Look you guys, since I made it and I'm the bartender, I'll name it. I once heard my daddy say the name of a drink that beats tha hell outa any thing ya'll have come up with...It's a 'Singapore Sling'."

So it was named.

"OK Bush," said Billy Bob, "Since you named it, how bout you goin upstairs an gettin some cigarettes for us to smoke with it."

Immediately, we all backed Billy Bob with our; "Unhuhs."

It was clear Bush didn't like it, but he got up and went back upstairs. This time he was gone longer. When he came back, he held his hand out and opened it; there were four half cigarettes and one whole one which he immediately put in his mouth, "The halves are yours, take it or leave it!"

We took our halves, then we all lit up and Bush poured the drinks, about four tablespoons each. With that, we sat down on the soft cushions, leaned back, and, like soldiers of fortune in a Bogart film, smoked our cigarettes and sipped our martinis.

Ten seconds later: coughs, gags, hacking, red faces and a lot of "Damns" filled the room. And the Bogart film ground to a halt.

When we finished spitting into the bar's sink we got some soap and washed our mouths out, to remove the slightest trace of

Singapore Sling. We smelled each other's breaths until we were certain our mothers could not pick up the slightest scent of our sin. To get Billy Bob back for destroying our skeleton, Bush and I told him we could still smell a little alcohol on his breath, so he should wash his mouth a second time.

In our church, drinking alcohol was right up there with murder, fornication, mixed swimming and dancing. It could send you straight to hell. Billy Bob, TC and I didn't have one of those places like Bush and Double M had where you could hang around for a while — we just went straight on to hell. Of course, all of us were going to end up in hell on earth if our mothers found out we'd been drinking and smoking.

After we'd cleaned up all the traces of our binge, we still had a couple of hours before the Millers returned home. We went to the second floor and began to systematically look in all the drawers and closets, with particular attention given to the room of Bush's older sister.

We saved the attic for last. It was narrow and long and smelled of mothballs. It was full of stuff: winter clothes, Christmas decorations, boxes of cards, letters and photographs, luggage, and more boxes on top of boxes.

Halfway into the attic, a glint of light above me caught my eye. I looked up. Two shelves ran the length of the right side of the room. On the highest shelf I could see the edge of a silver strip of metal. I pointed to it, "Bush, what's that?"

He looked and in a rather off handed tone said, "O that, that's my father's Knights of Columbus sword."

I almost fainted, *O my God, that's what Mr. Miller is going to use to cut my daddy's head off with.* I could feel my left eyelid twitching; all my breath caught in my throat; I might not breath or speak again.

Bush turned around and looked at me, "What's wrong with you? Are you sick? You better not vomit in here."

Billy Bob punched me in the back. It hurt like hell but started me to breathing and talking again, "Can I see the sword?"

"Yeah, but you got to swear on your mother's grave not to vomit."

"I swear on her grave." I said.

Bush looked at Billy Bob, "Can you reach it?"

Billy Bob was a full head taller than me. He was the tallest of all of us and lean as a beanpole. He stood on his toes, stretched his long arms and fingers; all of him was just enough to reach the sword's scabbard and lift it down.

Bush took it from him, gripped the handle and pulled the sword from its scabbard and held the blade up to the ceiling light. It glistened like Excalibur.

The second I saw it; I knew it could cut my father's head off. It was long, silvery and sharper than hell. I wanted to hold it. But before I could ask, Bush slid the sword back into the scabbard and gave it to Billy Bob, who put it back on the shelf.

Then, it was time to go home.

As the years passed we went our separate ways. The Millers moved away first, then TC and his family; after Billy Bob and Double M graduated from high school and went off to college, we might run into each other ever year or so. We'd talk a few minutes and make promises to get together and bring each other up to date. We never did. I made new friends, as I'm sure they did. Slowly I forgot them. But then, a few years back, when I started writing they suddenly came into my mind. I wrote a story about the five of us called *Pony*, followed by *Ride To Glory* and *Would You Give An Eye To See A...?* and now, as I write *The Sword In The Attic*, I see us clearly again: half naked, sitting around our 'Cussin' Tree', smoking and telling our newest dirty jokes; driving our soap-box racers through cardboard walls of fire; riding the lost pony that was the color of pure gold; and I hear our laughter and 'Damnations' as we shoot one another on our bare backs with rubber-guns; and, for a little, while we are together again.

Apaches

(TELEGRAM)

MESCALERO AGENCY, TO COMMISSIONER INDIAN AFFAIRS, WASHINGTON, D. C. AUG. 21ST 1879, WARM SPRING. INDIANS HAVE ALL LEFT THIS RESERVATION GOING WEST. WILL PROBABLY TRY TO INTERCEPT THOSE SUPPOSED TO BE ON THE WAY FROM SAN CARLOS. HAVE INFORMED THE MILITARY.

RUSSELL, AGENT

"These hills are full of Apaches. They've burned every ranch in sight. He had a brush with them last night. Says they're stirred up by Geronimo."

The first words in the movie *Stagecoach* — 1939

"They are the keenest and shrewdest animals in the world, with the added intelligence of being human beings."

Major Wirt Davis — 1885

"When they scalped an enemy they sang one song over it, a special song. The song goes on, "I will get a piece of the enemy's ribs, and I will get a piece of the enemy's backbone for me."
Western Apache Raiding and Warfare
— 1971

"I was born on the prairie where the wind blew free and there was nothing to break the light of the sun. I was born where there were no enclosures."

Geronimo

"I have killed ten white men for every Indian slain."

Cochise

"This could be good land without the Apaches."
From the movie *Chatto's Land* — 1972

On the hottest day of summer, when the sun was directly overhead and scorching the earth, heat waves created images of distant lakes. Everyone was asleep, even the soldiers; no one saw us or heard us; we broke away from our reservations and moved across the earth like the wind.

Of course, our mothers—the reservation agents—knew we were gone, for we had to have their permission to go out and play. Once outside, we became our true selves: marauding, pillaging, burning, wholly irreclaimable, savage killers. Filled with the power of the grizzly and the cunning of coyotes we were five bloodthirsty Apaches on the warpath.

We ran as fast as our legs would carry us to our camp beneath a large mock-orange tree. A thick wild-shrub hedge encircled the camp. It shielded us from any "White Eyes" that might be in pursuit. Normally, we called the tree the "Cussin' Tree" but on this day, Billy Bob said it was to be the "Sacred Tree." He was twelve and the oldest. He could probably have beat up any two of us together at one time. As always, he assumed leadership without any discussion or hint of dissent.

There was one problem about Billy Bob. And it was a big one. He had no eyebrows. They still hadn't grown back since they were burned off the month before. On that day he had convinced us to ride our Red-Rider wagons through a cardboard wall of fire. Having no eyebrows took away some of his ferocity. But only "some" because even though it made his face look a little like an owl I knew he could still kill me with his bare hands.

We sat cross-legged in a circle. Billy Bob stood above us. He began by giving us our names —

"Of course, I'm the only one who can be *Geronimo*.

"TC, you'll be *Cochise*.

"Double M, you're *Chatto*.

"Bush, you're *Victorio*.

"An' Spain, you'll be *Loco*."

"I don't want that name," I said.

"Well, since you're the craziest one of us...it fits." smirked Billy Bob.

Double M, who didn't even live on our street sniggered and I kicked him and we both drew back and likely would have gotten into it if Billy Bob hadn't ordered, "Damnit, you two, cut it out!"

"Well, I still don't like it," I said.

With that, Billy Bob, who was a good head taller than me, stepped over, leaned down and stuck his freckled face into mine, and in a voice that had a fist in it, said, **"Did you hear what I said? You're Loco an' I'm Geronimo, an' I'm tellin' you to quit whinin'! Loco killed a grizzly with a knife an' was a chief too, just not nearly as famous as Geronimo. You're Loco, got it?"**

"Un-huh."

"One more thing, every time ya'll talk to someone, use their Apache name. OK, that's settled...now get your stuff out."

One by one, we reached into our pockets and paper bags and pulled out what we had pillaged from our homes. We set our loot on the ground in front of us.

"Cochise, did you get the paint?"

"Yea, my sister's toothpaste."

"Chatto, what about the tobacco?"

"Yea, five of my granma's Lucky Strikes."

"Victorio, since your folks are the only ones that drink a lot, did you get the firewater?"

"I got it, but sure as hell my Daddy's gonna know 'cause I had to put an awful lot of water back in the bottles so he wouldn't see how much was gone."

"OK, Loco, what about you?"

I reached into the brown paper bag and pulled out a big handful of white feathers.

There was silence.

"Damn, was white all you could get?" rasped Billy Bob.

"Well, White Leghorns are all we've got in the pen an' I almost couldn't get them 'cause the rooster like to of spurred me to death pullin' his tail feathers out."

"Well, dad blast it, if you couldn't have got some Rhode Island Reds it seems the least you could have come up with was some Dominickers...Ah, hell! Pass out the

Leghorns…Give me that big one." He stuck it between the bandana and the back of his head. The rest of us did the same.

"OK, ya'll, look at these pictures I tore out of National Geographic at the library an' do your faces with a white streak across your noses an' cheekbones."

Billy Bob was a nut about Apaches and when it came to Geronimo he was a certified nut. He'd read everything he could get his hands on in libraries, the National Geographic and comic books. He had seen every movie that had an Apache in it. And he had a photographic memory of everything he had read or seen about them.

"Listen, ya'll! Geronimo was a Chiricahua Apache, so that's what we are. We're Chiricahuas. We're the fiercest of all Injuns."

I leaned over to Bush who was sitting beside me, "Did you hear that dirty word he just said we are?" I whispered the word in his ear.

Bush began giggling loudly and couldn't stop.

"So what's so funny Victorio?" hissed Billy Bob.

"Well, Spain, uh...I mean, Loco, uh, said you just said a dirty word."

"What'n hell, are you talkin' about?

"He said, you said, we are **Cheer-we-ca-cas.**"

With that TC fell over sideways on the ground and Double M started slapping his thighs and we all burst out laughing like hyenas—except for Billy Bob, whose neck was blood red with anger. He was so angry he was about to start bleeding from his nose. And he was silent. And when he got silent we got nervous. His jaw muscles twitched. His mouth was tight as a knife blade. His voice shook. **"Loco, I'm very near to scalping you!"** As he spoke his eyes became slits. His hand went down to the Boy Scout knife scabbarded on his belt.

"OK, OK," I said. "Loco speaks with forked tongue." I think it helped saying, "forked tongue" because the red in his neck went from bloody red to faint pink. The hand on the knife reached into a leather satchel that hung from his left shoulder. He took out a pipe. It was beautiful. The bowl was small and simple. It was made of red stone. The wooden stem was as long as my forearm; two Red Bird wings, tied to a short leather strap, hung from the stem.

He took the satchel off, laid it on the ground, placed the pipe on it and said, "This is our war pipe. It will give us power. Now, the White Eyes have come. They spread across our land like locusts. They kill us. We will not let this happen for we are Apaches. After we have smoked the pipe we will drive them back. Follow me. I will paint your faces for war. I will sharpen your weapons. I will gather horses an' guns. Then, they cannot stand against us."

At that moment, as the words came from his mouth, Billy Bob turned fully into Geronimo. As he called us to join him in driving the White Eyes from our land we answered with war whoops.

We were barefoot and wearing only shorts in front of which we had tucked white dishtowels so that they hung down like breechclouts. In those days, in the summer, the bottoms of kids' feet were tough as horses' hooves. We all had red bandanas tied around our foreheads.

Billy Bob pulled a black and white photograph from the satchel and held it up. We leaned forward. There were five Indians in a line: one was a baby; the other four were men; two of the men were in the center on horseback. "I'm the cruel lookin' one on the horse with a blaze. See those white stripes across their noses an' cheeks? That's lightnin'. Cochise gimme the paint." TC handed him the tube of toothpaste. "Now, I'm goin' to get ya'll ready for war. Chatto, lean over toward me."

One at a time, Billy Bob put a streak of white toothpaste across our faces. When he finished, we looked at one another. "Hell, Billy...I mean Geronimo, that's not half bad." said Double M. As he talked he squnched his face up trying to look mean. "How do I look?"

"Bad...real bad, like a Cherry...What is it we are?" asked Bush.

"**CHIRICHAUA!** Can't ya'll remember anything?" slashed Billy Bob.

I looked around. Everyone's face had hardened, our hair was longer and black; mouths were thin lines, eyes showed no mercy, skins were dark and tough as leather; we were transformed by another of Billy Bob's heroic visions. But, more had to happen before we swept down out of the hills without warning to raid the unsuspecting ranchers. There were more ceremonies to perform: the sharing of blood...and the smoking of the war pipe.

"Chirichauas, you are my people. We are of one blood!" As he spoke he pulled the knife from the scabbard, touched its point to his thumb, then; in a voice I had never heard before, except in movies when something serious was about to happen, something so serious it made you hold your breath, he said, "We will share our blood." And with that he began making a small cut on his thumb and then on the others each time pressing his thumb against theirs.

When he came to me I looked away as he cut my thumb. Then I fainted. I fell over sideways. Someone splashed water on my face and pulled me upright.

I shook my head. "Damn, that hurt like a son-of-a-bitch." But I was proud. We had mixed our blood. Truly, we were now "Blood Brothers".

Then, Billy Bob bowed his head to the pipe and picked it up with both hands and raised it up to the sun. "Sun Father, bless your sacred war pipe We will breathe its breath in and blow it upward to you....Chatto, give me the sacred tobacco." Double M handed the five cigarettes over and Billy Bob slit the paper with his knife and one after the other pushed the tobacco down into the bowl. When he finished he held the pipe toward the sun. "Now Chatto, give me the sacred fire." Double M reached in the pocket of his shorts and took out two wooden kitchen matches and handed them to Billy Bob. We watched in silence. He lit a match, put it to the bowl and took three deep breaths. Immediately, smoke rose. He turned slowly and blew smoke in the six directions.

He passed the pipe around the circle; each of us blew smoke toward the sun. It came to me. I have asthma. I took a deep breath. For a second I thought I was going to pass out again. I coughed hard enough for my insides to come out. Bush began to pound my back; TC took a slug of water from his canteen and spit in my face.

Billy Bob Geronimo looked at me with disgust. We were no longer boys playing a game. We were Apache warriors following our leader, the great Geronimo. *We were the rulers of our world.* Geronimo rose on his toes, "Hear me now. All this land an' all that is in it is ours. Today, we will sweep across it. First, we must take up our weapons. They are in the 'Sacred Wickiup'. I will bring them to you an' place them in your hands."

He turned, bent down and entered the low opening of an oval shaped brush hut that stood beside the "Sacred Tree." In a moment, he came out with his arms wrapped around a gosh awful armful of what he called, "weapons." Mostly they looked like a bunch of sticks. "As War Chief, I will take the largest bow, four arrows an' one of the tomahawks." He laid the rest at his feet.

"Cochise, since you are the best shot next to me you, shall have this strong bow an' three arrows.

"Chatto, the third bow is yours with two arrows.

"Victorio, you get the longest spear an' the other tomahawk.

"Loco, this will be your spear."

"Damn, Geronimo...is that all I'm gettin'. That little thing ain't even got a point on it. It wouldn't kill a chipmunk much less a human being...Damn!"

"Well, you're the littlest an' that's all that's left."

I was about to cry. He could see it. "OK Loco, remember you're a warrior. I'll let you choose where we're going to raid."

"Really...Me?"

"Yeh."

Oh my gosh! My mind raced. Who had something we wanted? What could we get away with and not get caught and killed by our parents? Who in the neighborhood did we dislike the most? Who did I dislike the most? The words jumped from my mouth.

"BROTHER BLACK!"

A few weeks before, Brother Black, a Church of Christ preacher, had embarrassed me terribly in front of Bush and Double M, both Catholics. TC, Billy Bob and I were Church of Christers. We went to Lipscomb, a

Church of Christ school where Brother Black taught. He knew us, especially me, since he sometimes preached at our church. Next to his house, which was only two streets away from where I lived, he owned a large field where he boarded people's horses.

On the day of my humiliation we had caught a lost pony on the Lipscomb campus and needed somewhere to keep her until we found the owner. I was certain Brother Black would help us out so I volunteered to go to the front door and ask him. Being as he was a preacher I knew he would say, "Absolutely boys, turn her loose in the field and come ride her anytime you want until you find her owner. I've got a pony saddle and bridle you can use. Is there anything else you need?"

But on that hot summer day, with a big smile on his beaming, righteous face, that Man of God looked down on us, and in his best preacher-voice said, "A dollar a day, boys, a dollar a day. That's what I charge everybody, and to be fair to everybody that's what I'll have to charge you."

I stumbled away, my head hanging down, muttering, "No, thanks...no thanks." We didn't have a dollar a week among us. Sixty-five years later, the bitter taste of that rejection remains fresh in my mouth. But on the day it happened my mind was saying as my feet drug me away, *'I'll get you back, Brother Butt Hole!'*

Now, my time had come.

"So, what's this about Brother Black?" asked Geronimo.

I jumped to my feet and shook my spear in the air. **"Ha-ya! We'll set his horses free to run with the wind. We'll take revenge on that White Eye for shaming us. Ha-ya! Blood for Blood! Ha-ya!"**

"Well, Damn, Loco!" Geronimo stepped back and stared at me like I was someone else. *I was.* Apache blood burned in my veins. I was ready to strike our enemy. I could see in Billy Bob's eyes that he was seeing that day again and was hearing that preacher say, *A dollar a day, boys, a dollar a day.* His eyes narrowed then expanded red with blood. He stared straight up into the sun. He seemed to grow taller and stronger. He began to stomp the ground hard, first with one foot then the other. His voice chanted —

Ha-ya Ha-ya Ha-ya Ha-ya Ha-ya
The sun's horse is a yellow stallion;
His nose, the place above his nose, is of haze,
His ears, of the small lightning, are moving back and forth,
He has come to us.
The sun's horse is a yellow stallion,
A blue stallion, a black stallion;
The sun's horse has come to us.

When he said, "The sun's horse has come to us" the first time, we came alive with his vision; we jumped to our feet and began stomping the ground, turning in circles, shaking our weapons above our heads, repeating with him the second time, "The sun's horse has come to us. We are ready. We are Apache. Hear Geronimo. He speaks!"

"Cochise, Victorio, Chatto, you will drive them toward us. Go to the the far end of the pasture. Loco and I will slip up to the house to see if any White Eyes are there. If none are , I will signal you with the cry of the hawk three times, **'EEEEEEEEE!'** When you hear it, climb the fence, spread out an' run screaming at the horses an' drive them toward the house. We will open the gate."

Except for the hawk screech, which was more like a girl being strangled, it sounded like a good plan.

We ran from tree trunk to tree trunk toward Brother Black's house. Both of us were now calling him "Brother Butt Hole." There was no car in the driveway or garage. Geronimo signaled me to stay behind a tree. Stooping as low as he could he ran across the lawn and peered over one windowsill after another. Then—and I couldn't believe he was doing it—he stepped up onto the front porch and knocked on the door, not once, but twice. No one came.

With that, he motioned to me and we walked out into the side yard, which sloped to the pasture below. We could see the horses—there were eleven of them. At the far end of the field was the fence where the other warriors awaited Geronimo's signal. The signal came—

EEEEEEEE EEEEEEEE EEEEEEEE

With a final screeching scream, Geronimo began to cough, wheeze and damn. He sounded like me having an asthma attack. I slapped him on the back. He wheeled around, "Damn you, Loco, cut that out!"

From below, we heard war cries. Running across the pasture like devils, three warriors rushed toward the grazing horses, leaping, whooping, shouting and shaking their weapons. The horses threw their heads up, snorted, reared and wheeled in the air and broke into a gallop straight toward us. Before they reached the slope, Geronimo threw the gate open and yelled to the top of his voice, **" Ha-ya Ha-ya Ha-ya! The sun's horse has come to us!"**

And there was another voice mixed with Geronimo's, **"Ha-ya Ha-ya Ha-ya! The sun's horse has come to us!"** At first, I couldn't tell where it was coming from then I realized it was coming from me.

Pounding the earth, the horses came pouring up the slope. In a cloud of dust they galloped through the open gate and out onto the street. Not far behind, running harder than I had ever seen them, were Cochise, Victorio and Chatto; their faces unrecognizable with wildness; the white toothpaste melting down their cheeks, they passed me, racing behind the horses whose hooves on the asphalt street cracked like rifle shots.

We were transformed back in time and space. Our feet did not touch the earth. Our minds, our bodies enlarged with blood. No human, no animal could stop us. Like wolves we veered in and out of scrub brush, cactuses, boulders, mesas and canyons; all was desert and air and the black stallions and blue stallions and yellow stallions blew and snorted ahead of us, their manes and tails streaming in the air behind them. We ran on and on, hollering and yelling — the horses — the Apaches — the sun — all together as one.

Then came a jolt of horns, a screeching of brakes and angry shouts. And in an instant we were all back in the real world.

All but one...

Billy Bob was standing in the middle of Granny White Pike jumping up and down and hollering, **"I was born on the prairie where the wind blows free. I was born where there were no enclosures. I was born..."** He stopped, looked around; his face flushed. He was confused, "Where am I...where is everybody?" His mouth clamped shut. For a moment he stood still as a statue, you could see reality returning horribly to him. He shuddered but didn't move from where he stood. He was lost. We looked at him...then we walked side-by-side out into the street as though the cars and horns and people and shouts were not there. We closed around our friend and leader and without a word led him across the street onto the Lipscomb campus—where the horses were now quietly grazing.

Exhausted, we plopped down on the grass near the horses. Bush and TC had their canteens. They poured water on Billy Bob's face and head. As he sputtered and cooled he gradually became himself again—almost—but not completely. His normal domineering voice and manner were completely gone. If you had not known him in the fullness of his normality you would say, 'Damn, that boy's awfully low on spunk, ain't he?' Mostly he just stared into the distance. When we asked him if he was OK he just shrugged or said a word or two so low you couldn't understand him.

Finally, TC pointed at him, "Golly, guys, look at Billy Bob's eyes, they've got that 'thousand-yard stare' just like the ones you see in soldiers eyes in *Life*. Sure as hell, he's shell-shocked. We better get him home to his mama before he starts runnin' in circles an' screamin'."

But nobody moved. We were sitting there remembering the day Billy Bob went home with his eyebrows burned off. That night's punishment was stuck in our minds forever. That night, our mothers called one another and shared their child's confession. By suppertime we had all been whipped with hands, switches, belts and anything that didn't break bones or permanently mar flesh or soul for life.

What were we to do? Our leader had turned to mush.

And then...and then, like the Day of Judgment, Brother Black stood above us with the Wrath of God on his face. Behind him stood several men in suits who looked like God's avenging angels.

I do not want to tell you what happened to us.

Kings X and Time Out

Kings X and time out
Where are the back slapping lads
Who rolled me down the bumpbacked hills
When I was King on the mountain
With always a shout in my heart?

Where are those blind-man bluff days
When Jacks were nimble and quick
And never a dragon was feared
As I straddled my fathers shoulders
With never a rhyme in my mind

That our London Bridged Summers were falling
And all our Happy Humpty Dumptys
Were breaking never again to rise
And all the saints who patty-caked were growing
With forever a remembering in my heart.

Would You Give An Eye To See A…?

It was our very last Friday before the end of summer vacation; our last three days of freedom; our last three days before we returned to the fiery pit; our last three days before our parents forced us back to school.

There were five of us. Billy Bob was twelve and the oldest. He had fast fists and was our leader. TC, Bush and Double M were eleven. I was ten, the youngest, and the follower. Bush and Double M were Catholic, the rest of us Church of Christ.

We were sprawled on the ground beneath the 'Cussin' Tree.' Hidden from the spying eyes of grown ups by wild hedges and bushes; it's where we went to smoke and talk ugly and plot and scheme against the unfair rules of grownups. It's also where we learned from one another some of the facts of life, wonderfully distorted though they so often were. We'd just finished a close examination of the Women's Underwear section in the Sears Roebuck Catalogue I had brought and were smoking away on the Camels Billy Bob had confiscated from his father. Everyone's face was serious.

"Well, we'd better make tha best outta tomorrow," said Bush.

"Damn right bout that," said TC.

"Double damn right bout that," said Double M.

"Well we better come up with somethin good, cause ya'll know what comes after tomorrow," I said.

Except for school days, Sunday mornings were the most horrible part of the week. God could have done a whole lot better when He made it. Every Sunday morning we had to pay for our sins of smoking, lying, stealing, cursing and for — well you know — what boys do at night under the covers. Penance began with: scrubbed faces, slicked down hair, starched shirts, itchy suits and ties so tight they could have strangled a Silverback Gorilla to death.

Church was ninety percent boredom and ten percent pure terror. Most preachers weren't worth a tinker's damn when it came to holding a kid's attention. But it's sort of funny, for the older I've gotten the more appreciation I've had for all those years of being bored to death in church. I think it helped me out in life. During the half an hour the preacher was droning on and on I would sit there dreaming up all kinds of stuff in my head that might keep me out of school for a few days: things like breathing in a lot of dust and having an attack of asthma, or drinking enough soapy water to make myself vomit, or getting a dog to bite me. Church was a hothouse that helped my imagination grow.

Then there were those ten percent times of terror. These were usually during revivals. Revivals were held at least once a year, more often if the elders thought the congregation's attention wasn't focused enough on the Final Judgment or that the numbers were slipping on baptisms and restorations. They'd bring in some fire and brimstone big name that could scare the daylights out of adults and terrorize the children. He'd get so worked up you could taste sulfur in the air and see the Devil's face reflecting in his eyes. Sometimes I couldn't look I'd get so scared. A couple of times I wet my bed at night.

My preference was stories from the Old Testament; those filled with throwing people to lions, walls of water drowning millions of Egyptians, dogs eating women, and Samson killing a ton of Philistines with the jawbone of an ass. These kept me wide-awake with my eyes and ears glued on the preacher. But I paid for it at night. The sounds and pictures of all that screaming and blood and death would creep into my bedroom and scare me so bad I'd cover my head with the sheet and pray out loud until I fell asleep. I think these gory sermons influenced my later love of horror stories and movies and some of my own gory writings. So church wasn't entirely wasted on me.

Thank the good Lord my family was Church of Christ. If they'd been Catholic I would have been dead before I was eight years old. I had asthma. Breathing all that smoke pouring out of those little buckets the priests swung around and around over everybody's head would sure as anything smothered me to death right there in my pew. And as to being an alter boy — un uh — dressing up like a girl in a long white gown and carrying big, tall things and chanting in Latin would have been worse than what I up against in church.

Speaking of Latin, I need to say something about its affect on my life. I tried it out for two years in high school and for two years it gave me a splitting headache. I suffered just like the saying goes, "Latin is a dead language, as dead as can be. First, it killed the Romans, now it's killing me." It would have been easier on my brains to have pounded my head against a rock as against Caesar's *Gallic Wars.* I made two years of straight Ds. When I reminded Ms. Whitten, my Latin teacher, of this at our fiftieth high school reunion she tried to reassure me with the comforting words, "But George, they were all good Ds."

So there we were under the Cussin' Tree trying to come up with a good plan for living it up on Saturday. One dumb idea after another had been shot down when TC who was leaning back on his elbows sat up, took a deep draw off his cigarette and said, "I'll tell you what we outta do, there's a double feature at tha Princes an they're showing *Strangler Of The Swamp* and *Isle Of The Dead* with Boris Karloff...Man, ya can't beat Karloff for our last day on earth together." TC, was prone to speak in extremes and loved horror movies more than he loved his little sister. He saw he had our attention. He took another deep draw, paused dramatically, looked slowly around at each of us, then said, "Hell, ya'll know there's only one place for us to go…we gotta spend tha whole day downtown."

While he wasn't known for having good ideas, the moment TC said it we all knew he had knocked the ball out of the park. Downtown it was!

Downtown Nashville was our playground and one of our schools of life. We roamed it. We explored it. We tasted and smelled it. Nooks and crannies, every alley, every stairwell, every rooftop held something new; at times something disturbingly glorious and — now and then — we discovered something so horrible it returned in the dark of the night, hovering above our beds. The city was filled with blind musicians, beggars, all shades of colored people, parades of women with mink around their shoulders, men in pin striped suits and two-toned shoes, and a man without legs rolling down the sidewalk on a small wooden shelf attached to roller-skates.

If we didn't ride the bus to town, my father would drive us in one of his shiny Cadillacs to his car lot on Broad, two blocks from the heart of downtown. None of the other fathers had cars approaching anywhere near my dad's Cadillacs. He was a man to behold. He was big and prosperous looking. He wore a diamond ring. His fingernails were polished. His hair was oiled and slicked back; his suits, shirts, ties and shiny shoes were the finest and always immaculate. I took some pride in having a father who could have passed for a gangster where none of the other fathers could have. From his lot we headed into the heart of the city like a small band of Cherokee searching and hunting for whatever prey was unfortunate enough to cross our path.

First and foremost was Harveys, Nashville's largest and newest Department Store. It had everything: real live monkeys in a cage beside a soda fountain, a carousel, clowns and, most special of all, the city's first escalators. Six floors high, we could spend a good couple of hours there playing hide-and-go-seek, cramming all five of our bodies into elevators filled with the bodies of women shoppers, examining naked female mannequins and women's lingerie, and running up the escalators going down and down those going up.

From Harveys, we advanced, side-by-side, up the sidewalk to the State Museum beneath the War Memorial building. The Museum contained two of Tennessee's greatest possessions: big glass jars of formaldehyde with things in them — horrible things — that looked like babies. The other was an Egyptian mummy that was just a little older than our grandparents.

We could hardly take our eyes off the things floating in the jars.

Bush whispered, "Oh my gosh, are those real babies?"

"You dummy!" said TC, "Can't you see they ain't babies, they're aliens. I saw some that looked just like em in *Monsters From Mars*. My dad says they're everywhere out in New Mexico. Flying Saucers land out there all tha time an my dad says that tha government keeps it a big secret. These must have been some that got away an got run over on the highway an somebody from Tennessee found em and picked em up an contributed em to the Museum. Hell, they might even have come from somewhere up in tha Smokies. I bet they land up there too."

"Oh my gosh! I ain't ever goin to tha Smokies again."

"Yep, that's exactly what they are. They're aliens!"

Bush was beginning to look a little queasy, like he might throw up. I guess he would have if Billy Bob hadn't brought us back down to earth with a sharp finality, "Hellsfire-an-damnation ya'll, let's go look at tha mummy."

The mummy mesmerized Billy Bob. I believe he would have skipped going to a movie or eating Krystals just to stand there and stare at it — especially where its sex parts were, or at least where they should have been; as far as I could tell whatever had been there a million years before had dried up and fallen off. Every time he looked at it, his eyes would bulge and start shining and his face would turn red and now and then his body would quiver and every time he'd say the same thing, "Ya'll, look-a-there. Look-a-there. Look at his weenie. Look at his weenie!" And he'd be pointing with his finger and it would be jerking back and forth like it was going straight through the glass.

His voice would rise higher and higher and we'd tell him to hush up or a guard would come in. And one time one did. He stared at us for a minute then asked, "What's goin on here?" We were so scared nobody answered. I could see he was studying Billy Bob the hardest. I think he figured it all out quickly because he stuck his thumbs in his gun belt and nodded toward Billy Bob, "OK, you fellows get on outa here right now an be sure an take him with you. We don't want his type hangin around here." Double M and Bush got behind Billy Bob and shoved him ahead of us until we got outside. Once the sun and air hit him he began to come back.

Next stop was the State Capitol. While not quite as good as the Museum, it had its points. There was a real dead man named William Strickland in its walls. First thing we'd do was go to the exact spot where his bones, or whatever was in there, and put our ears up against the stone to see if we could hear anything. Then we'd put our hands on the stone to see if it was cooler than the others, for that was a sure sign a ghost or spirit was there.

Though horror movies sometimes made TC wet his bed he loved Poe as much as he loved Count Dracula and Frankenstein movies. Before he said it, I knew exactly what was going to come out of his mouth because I'd read everything Poe had written.

"I betcha he was buried alive in there!"

Double M leaned forward and put his ear against the stone. All of us held our breaths and watched. For a minute nothing happened then, his lips stretched away from his teeth, his eyes bulged, his face contorted and a guttural rasping came from deep in his throat. Bush was standing right beside me; I heard a faint voice, almost as though it had no breath, "Oh my gosh...Oh my gosh...that thing's in there an it's alive..."

Just as Bush said, "that thing's in there an it's alive", Double M shoved back away from the wall, leaped into the air with his face like a madman's, his hands like claws and screeched, **"YAAEEEeeeeee!"**

It scared me so bad I squnched my eyes and covered my face with my hands.

Then he began laughing loudly and I heard a 'thud.'

"Damn, that hurt!" cried Double M.

"Well that's for you bein a damn fool," said Billy Bob.

I took my hands away and opened my eyes.

Double M was rubbing his right shoulder where Billy Bob had hit him. TC was rising from a crouch where he had folded his arms over his head for protection. Bush was nowhere to be seen.

Ten minutes later we found him hiding in the Men's Restroom. For a bit he refused to come out of the stall. It took all of us to convince him that it was just another of Double M's sick jokes. Finally the stall door opened slowly and Bush peeked out. He looked both ways, seeing there was no moldy dead man in the room he stepped out. Glaring at Double M, he hissed, "You're sick." and walked out of the restroom.

Before we left the Capitol we went inside and took a quick look at the chipped place on the marble handrail beside the wide steps that led up to the Senate and House

Chambers; the crack was made by one politician shooting at another and missing. Every time we stuck our fingers in the crack we were disappointed no one had been killed.

From the Capitol we descended upon the Bennie Dillon building; it was twelve stories high. There were two things that drew us to that building every time we were downtown: the stairwell and the rooftop.

From the top floor of the stairwell was a ten-inch opening between the handrails all the way down to the ground floor. From the top floor you could see hands on the railing as people came up the steps. The goal was to spit and hit the hand. Nine out of ten times we missed but on the tenth, when you struck your target and heard the horrified scream of a woman or the loud cursing of a man, it was better than making an A in Latin. Because of my asthma and congestion I tended to have several gallons more mucous than the others, thereby I was, hands down, the champion spitter — it was usually my spit that hit.

If you hit a man as old as Methuselah or one with a bad leg all you'd get was a lot of ugly language, but if you hit a man who could still run up steps the next thing you'd hear was pounding footfalls as he came tearing upward shouting, "When I catch you I'm going to rip your mouth out then I'm going to kill you."

Then, like Bush, at the Capital, we would flee to the nearest restroom and hide in the stalls, even if we all had to cram into one. There we waited: not breathing, not talking, praying silently; after a half a day or so, if it was quiet, we'd send the one who'd hit the hand out to see if the assassin was gone. If so, we'd go back and spit awhile more until our spit ran out. Then we would go to the rooftop.

We knew almost every unoccupied part of the Bennie Dillon Building. The rooftop was the most special spot of all. From there you could see the river and barges, the distant tree covered hills; leaning over the low brick wall at the edge you could see the shoppers, they scurried back and forth like ants, in and out of holes, twisting their antennas, telling one another where they had just bought this or that, or had just eaten that or this, and then they scurried on to other holes and other ants.

As there was a strong desire within me to live I was terrified about standing anywhere near the edge of anything over twelve feet high. Twelve stories into the sky was the next thing to being on Everest without any ropes around you. The nearer I got to the edge of the rooftop the more my imagination took hold. A malignant force drew me forward. To avoid being called 'chicken' I would ease up to it, barely lifting my feet, and look over the side then quickly step back. In that one glance down through the clouds to the earth far below I could see myself toppling over that little bitty, frail wall and screaming for thirty minutes before I hit the sidewalk. And I could hear my dear mother weeping and see my father shaking his head at the stupidity of his idiot son.

Billy Bob was in the lead as we climbed the last steps to the door that opened onto the roof. As he put his hand on the knob he turned and looked at me, "Well Spain, are you going to jump this time?" He, like the rest of us, had a twisted sense of humor. The others laughed, I looked at my feet, as Billy

Bob's hand turned the knob and the door began to open.

At this point, I need to pause and explain about a game we played at the Cussin' Tree. We'd be lying on the ground around it, leaning back on our elbows, smoking and telling dirty jokes when all of a sudden one of us would say, "Hey ya'll, would you give an eye to see a...?" and then he'd say something so gross or obscene it can't be repeated here; if it was really awful we'd hold our noses and make gagging sounds. But if it was something so sexually graphic we could see it, we'd sit up and lean toward the speaker with our eyes stretched wide and excited and begin to talk all at once, "My gosh, say that all over again...Damnation that's, that's...Oh my, Oh my...Do you know anymore like that?" When you got that reaction you were hands down the gross subject champion for the day! And for certain, someone would say, "Well, I'd give an eye to see that."

Billy Bob pushed the door all the way open and, one-by-one, we stepped out into the bright sunlight. For a moment we couldn't see a thing and then, suddenly, we could see. *'Oh my goodness! Oh my goodness!'* was all my mind could say. My entire body filled with electricity. If souls can quiver I think mine quivered so hard it left my body.

For a boy and — a thousand times more for a man — there's nothing God placed on this earth that comes anywhere near equaling the body of a woman who is almost naked. It is absolutely why the words 'frenzied anticipation' were created. All we hoped for. All we prayed for. Our very reason for existing.

There before us, stretched out on a towel, was a woman sun bathing in her underwear.

I clamped my hands over my eyes so fast and hard I almost broke my nose. I stopped breathing. Time passed. There was a great silence. More time passed. And then I heard my voice speak to me in my head, *'Would you give an eye to see an almost naked woman?'* There was not the slightest hint of a pause as my voice answered, *'Yes! Oh yes!'* And as it spoke I said a quick prayer, opened my left eye…and peeped between my fingers.

Long years have passed since that glorious day of sunshine and still I quiver in frenzied anticipation when I see an almost naked woman with my two good eyes. Thank you God for your never-ending mercies!

Halloween 1946

And lead us not into temptation, but deliver us from evil.

For thine is the kingdom, and the power, and the glory forever. Amen

Matthew 6:13

But the Good Lord didn't deliver us! In fact He's the One ultimately responsible for Halloween. He's the One who approved the Devil's request to create a day "just 'especially for young boys and criminals." He's the one that backed the Devil up in setting October 31 as Halloween every year to scare the bejesus out of us. Somewhere in the Bible He admits it, "Know ye this, I created Halloween with the Devil's help to scare the hell out of you so ye would turn from your evil ways and turn back to Me to save your evil soul from the fiery depths."

Serious studies have been done by the Church of the Revelations in Hohenwald, Tennessee that prove — beyond all dispute — Halloween has brought multitudes of lost sinners back to the Lord. As always, we, the Cherokee Five, did our part to help Him out.

Think about this for a moment; five boys, ages 10 to 14, their faces covered with masks, roaming your neighborhood on Halloween night. It sort of gets your "on guards" perked up with thoughts of, *What'n hell kinda awfulness are they planning before this night's over.*

Billy Bob wore a bright, red Devil's mask that had hair like little flames coming out the sides and top. It must have cost a bundle 'cause it 'ud scare the you know what out of little children and scary types of grown ups.

TC thought he looked just like King Kong with his big black-faced gorilla mask. His neck got red and he clenched his fist when I said, "Doggone it TC you're a perfect monkey."

Double M said he was a goat but when he bleated through his mask he sounded like his throat was being cut.

Bush slipped his on and made a pretty good roaring sound which was supposed to be a grizzly. The only problem was the mask looked more like Lassie.

Mine was home made with bits and pieces of paper and cloth put together with scotch tape, strings and big rubber bands and painted all over. When I put it on, Billy Bob stepped back and grimaced, "The Lord have mercy, GE, what…what's that?"

"I'm gonna be a Crazy Clown." First, I'd painted the whole thing white then, put big red lips and cheeks in a smile like the "Joker's." The eyes were coal-black with large arching eyebrows. I liked what I saw in the mirror so I added a scar that came down from my left forehead, across my eye, ending below my cheek. When I came out of the bedroom my sisters screamed and ran out of the room and our dog tried to crawl under the couch — I knew I was ready.

We set out as it was turning from dusk to dark. All our parents told us to be home by 10:00 or they would come looking for us and several of them hinted at beatings if we did anything that might lead to neighbors threatening lawsuits or the police showing up with blue lights flashing.

We gathered in Billy Bob's backyard. Except for Bush carrying a silly plastic pumpkin bucket, the rest of us had brown grocery bags to put our treats in.

"OK guys, let's go get 'em," said Billy Bob.

We cut through the backyard hedge and the yard beyond to a brightly lit front porch of an old two-story house where we were greeted at the door by two obnoxious teenage boys who immediately began making fun of us. When Billy Bob blurted out "Trick or treat," the oldest one laughed, "Well treat this trick up yours," and shot us a finger and slammed the door in our face.

That was a big mistake.

Without a word we followed Billy Bob back around the house to the backyard to the goldfish pond with its concrete statue of a sweet, little child standing in the center. One after another we ringed ourselves around the pond, unzipped our pants, pulled ourselves out and pissed every drop of piss we had in us outward as far as we could go. It glittered in the moonlight. TC and Double M were our champion pissers. Both hit the statue. Someone must have struck a big goldfish right between its eyes, for it wasn't a second before one turned belly-up onto the surface.

After this most people were nice, filling our bags with candy and cookies and one lady even gave us a slice of pecan pie. We went out to the street, curved our bottoms down in a ditch and gorged: pie first, cookies second, ending with Goo Goos for desert. Then everyone got silent and laid back and looked up at the stars. "Damn, that's pretty," somebody muttered.

"Damn right 'bout that," said someone else.

"Wonder what's up there?" asked Bush.

"Hell Bush, don't they teach you anything at all at that St. whatever place it is you go to on Sunday? God's up there and heaven too."

"But where up there? All I can see are stars."

"I guess beyond 'em somewhere. Damn Bush, ask one of those Catholic guys that wears sheets an all that fancy stuff...Yeh see Bush that's one of the problems with Catholics, ya'll only sprinkle a little water on a baby's head an don't really dunk people all the way down under the water to the bottom when yeh baptize 'em…no wonder ya'll don't know doodly-squat 'bout God an heaven an stuff. Plus yeh have to eat fish every Friday 'til yeh die…Can't yeh see somethin' ain't right?"

Suddenly, Billy Bob jumped to his feet and out of the ditch announcin', "OK guys, it's gettin' on an' we got a bunch more houses to hit before goin' home…Let's go!"

No one was home in the next two houses so we hung their porch chairs up in trees. At the next door a little rat-like dog came growling out and grabbed ahold of my left pants leg and wouldn't let go. The beast's owner was a nice old lady who told him, "Stop that Hubbert, leave that nice boy alone," and picked him up and gave me an extra Hershey bar and a pat on the head.

We saved Brother Black's house for last. He was a preacher and teacher made out of flint and had turned us away once when we asked to put a lost pony we'd caught into his pasture. We'd fixed him then and I was ready to do it again if he acted like a craphead.

Every light was off. I knocked. No lights came on. No one opened the door. I knocked again — still nothing. "OK, let's all knock." We did — Nothing.

"OK, bang on it as hard as you can an' holler trick or treat as loud as you can."

We banged away and hollered, **"TRICK OR TREAT...TRICK OR TREAT...TRICK OR TREAT!"**

Suddenly the door flew open.

He stood there with a face of stone glaring down on us like the wrath of God. So he thought...so he thought. I stared upward straight into his eyes thinking, *'You ain't God. All you are is a mean old Craphead.'*

Still he stood there — silent — staring at us. Then, he raised his left arm with his hand toward our faces, "Get thee behind me you little Satan's!" And flicked his fingers at us as though we were insects and slammed the door so quick and hard he hit Bush's pumpkin bucket and cracked it, spilling candy everywhere.

We stood for a long moment almost bleeding from the corner of our eyes we were so angry. "Let's kill 'im," said Double M who liked Edward G. Robinson gangster movies.

"Un un, I brought somethin' for him," and pulled two strong clothesline cords out of my pocket and stretched them out tightly, "These 'ul fix old Craphead."

"Damn GE, I didn't really mean for us ta kill 'im."

"Ya'll follow me an' be quiet." I led them through the dark, opened the gate to the field and walked slowly toward the dark outlines of Black's four walking-horses as I reached into my sack and got some chocolate out.

The horses smelled it and came toward me. "Bush, get some chocolate and feed it to them while I go behind them an' do somethin'."

After I'd finished tying the horse's tails together I whispered, "OK, let's go home."

That night I slept the sleep of the righteous.

Ah! Summer begins, begins

And all is as it was before winter's wearing away
The sow bellied suns
Heigh-ho-hurrah, thrusting, swelling, kicking,
Meaning of it all,
The mercy in it all,
Adoring the mercy in us all
Crambling up the cradle's side shouting,
"It's lust that makes a man,
And dust is where he ends."
As all the black-blooded earth throbs, spreads and opens.
And the Sweat of Summer's
Sour, smelly, pitthighbrow
Plows deep into the blood-sweet earth Dripping, flooding beneath the moving grass
Swarming with wild-brown bees dancing tall tales
As they buzz their busy business with wild-brown boys
Who dare their devils above in trees and beneath the water falls

While the sun dries all their glory away,
And clouds climb and climb and collide into tomorrow
Then slide back again into today:
Wavering weaving in images walking on water;
While all the while the trod and throb of summer lifts
Old men and lambs upward into the sky
And there, for a little bit,
They stride upon their pride
Which never ends.

www.ingramcontent.com/pod-product-compliance
Lightning Source LLC
Chambersburg PA
CBHW030521080526
44586CB00011B/283